This Coloring Book
belongs to:

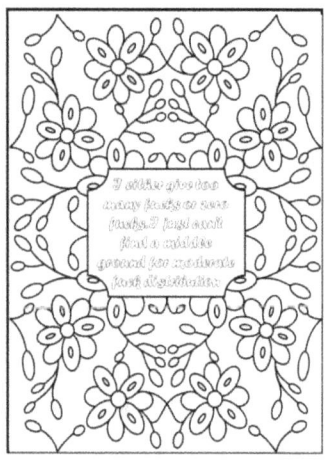
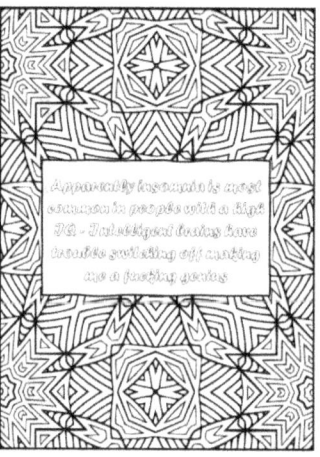
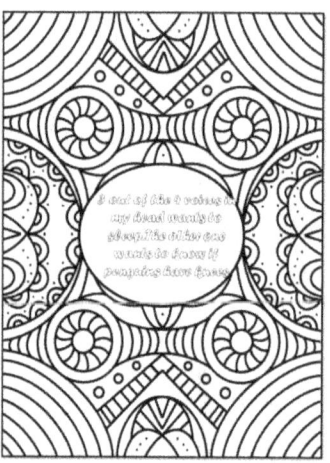

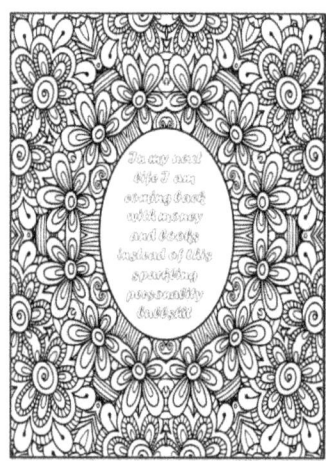
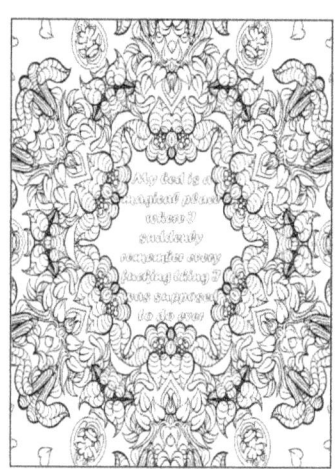

If you enjoy this book please consider leaving a favourable review on Amazon as it really helps out us small independent publishers (and makes us do a little happy dance)

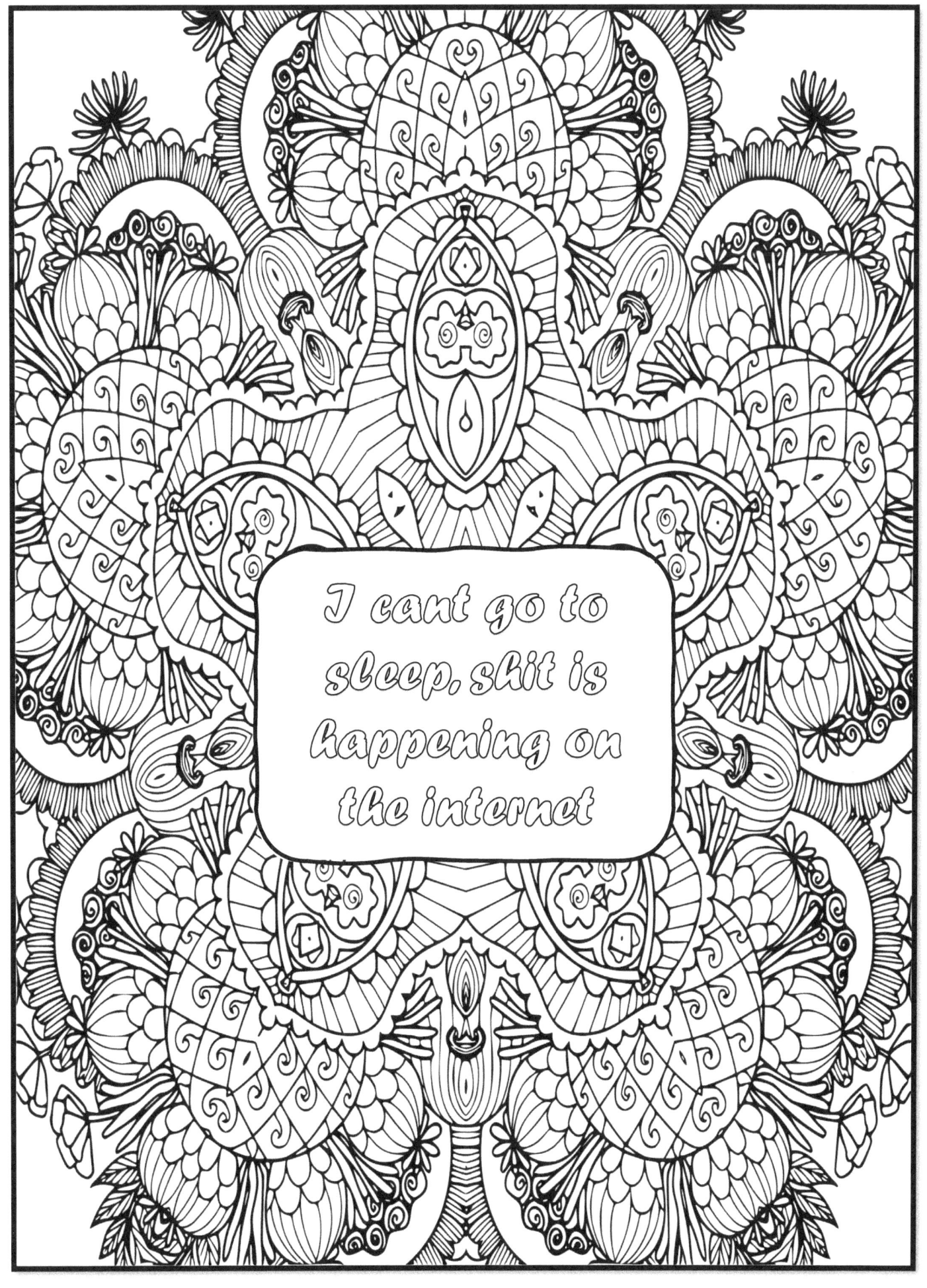

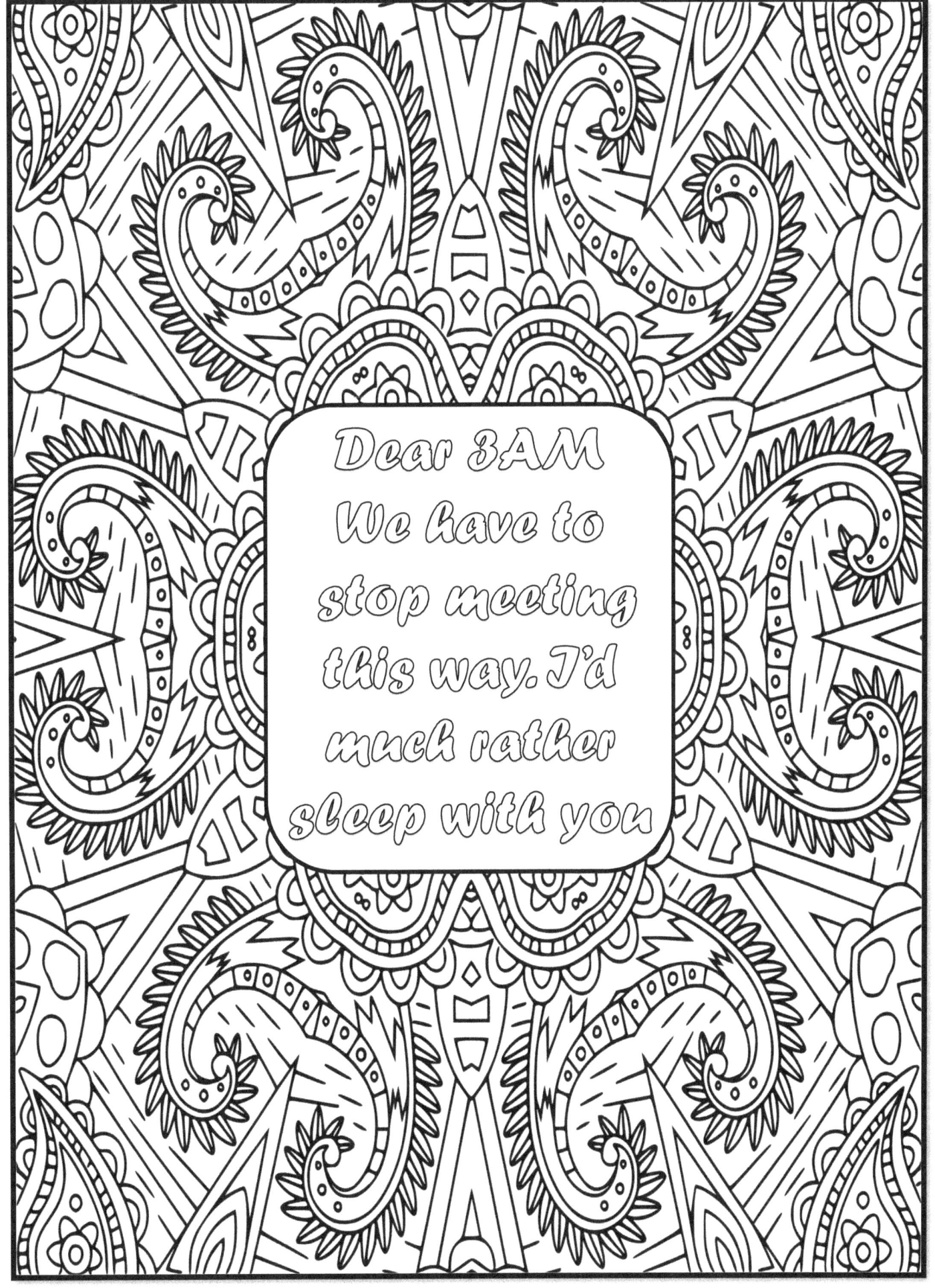

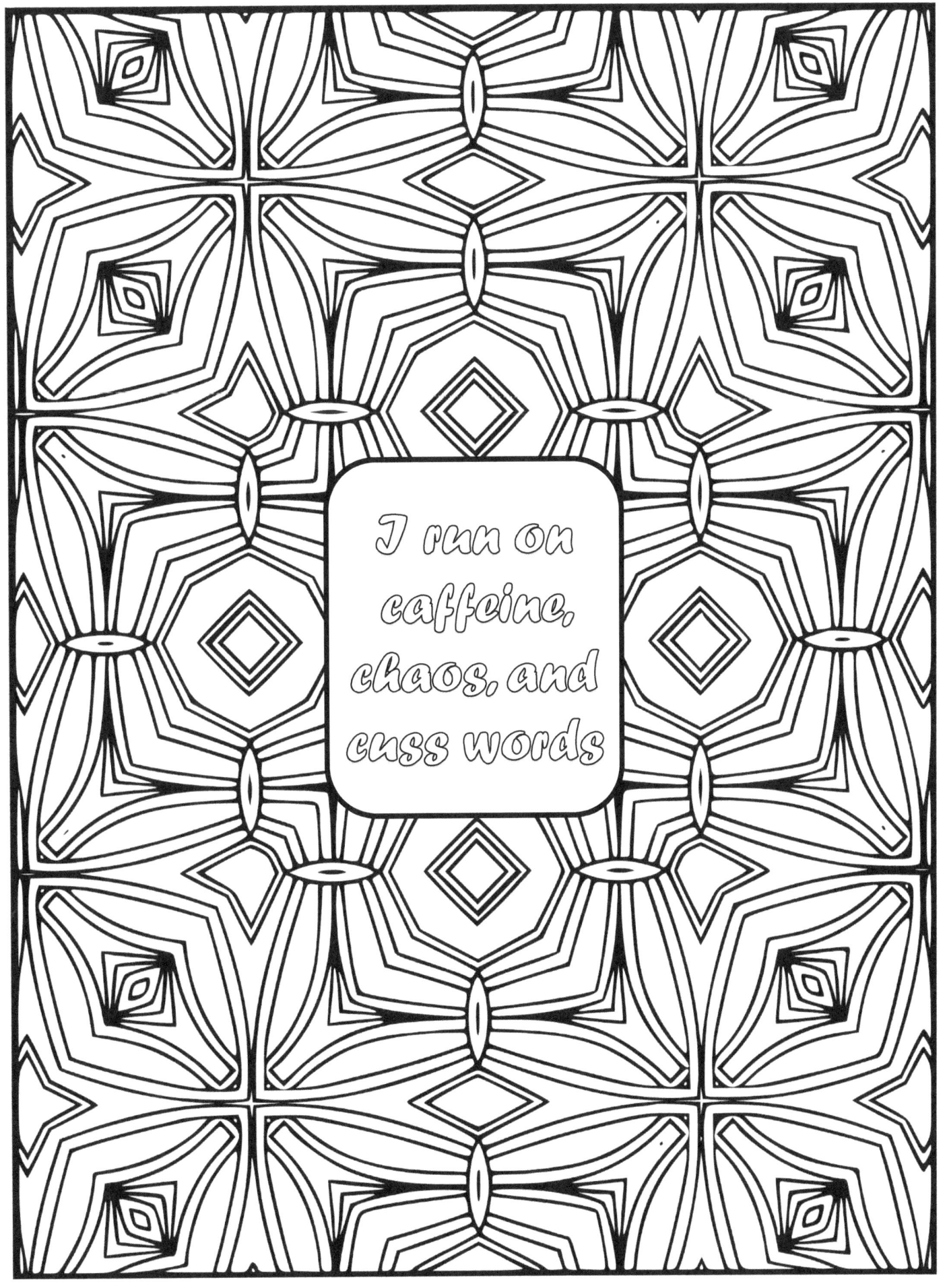

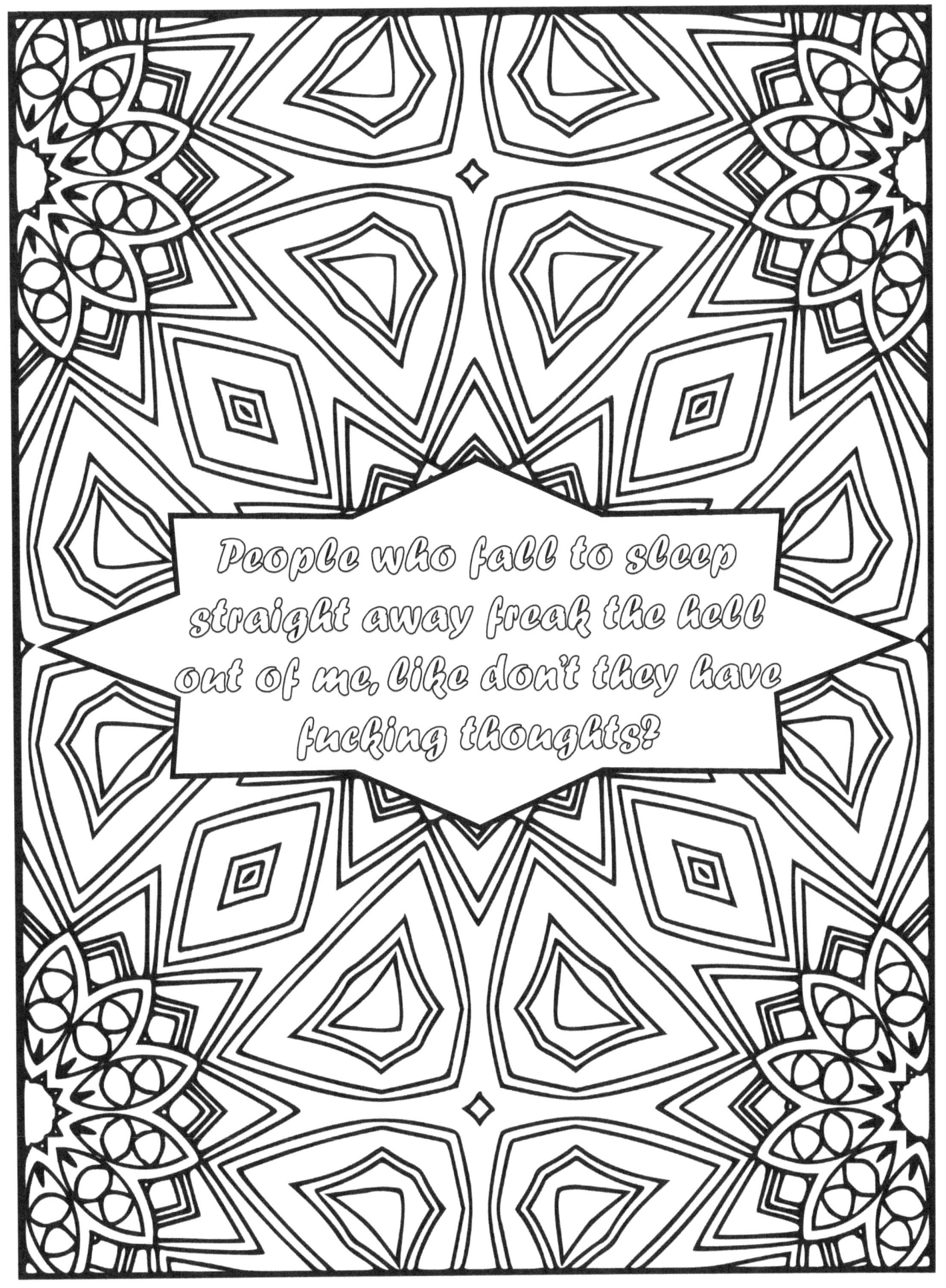

People who fall to sleep straight away freak the hell out of me, like don't they have fucking thoughts?

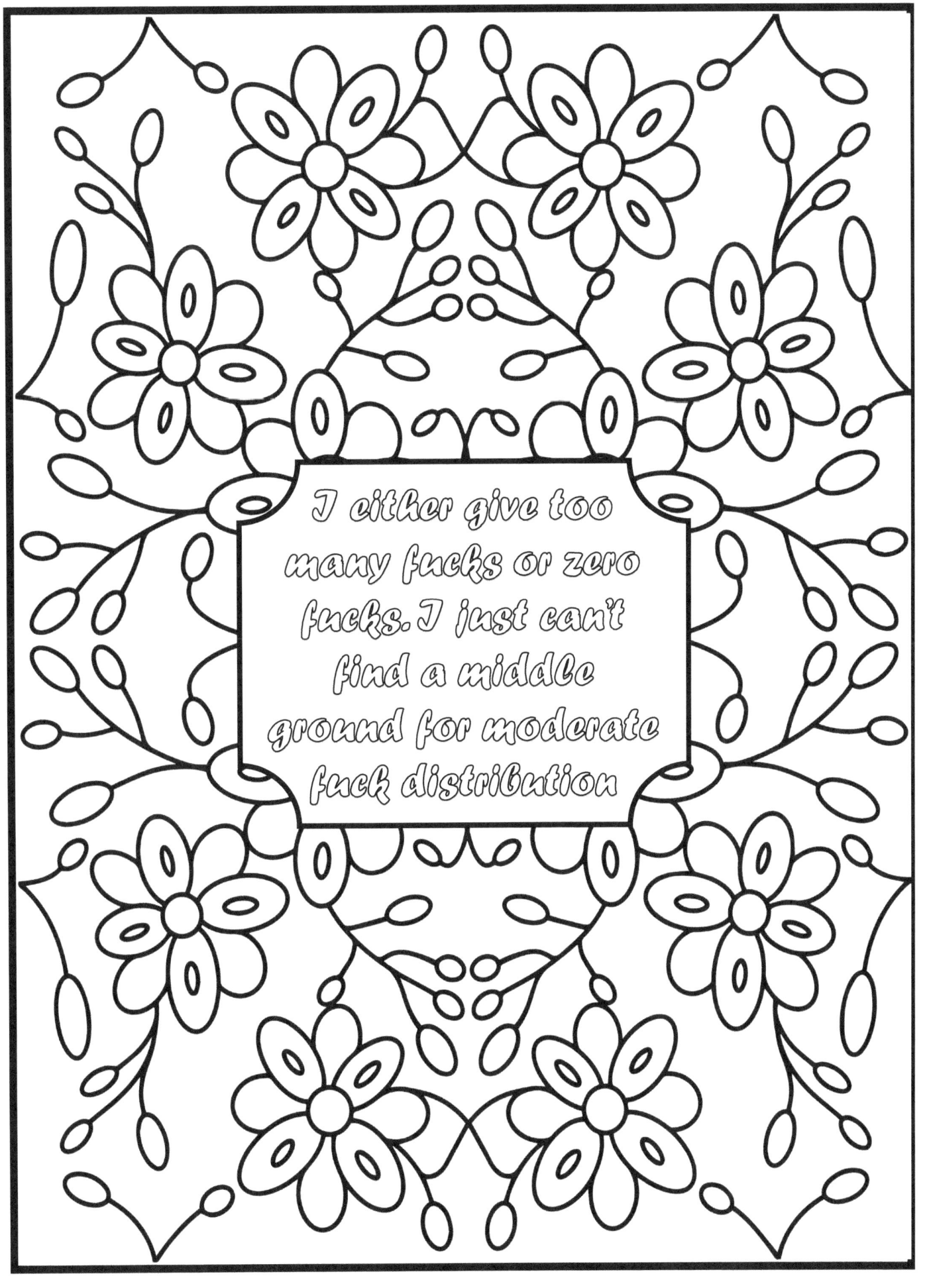

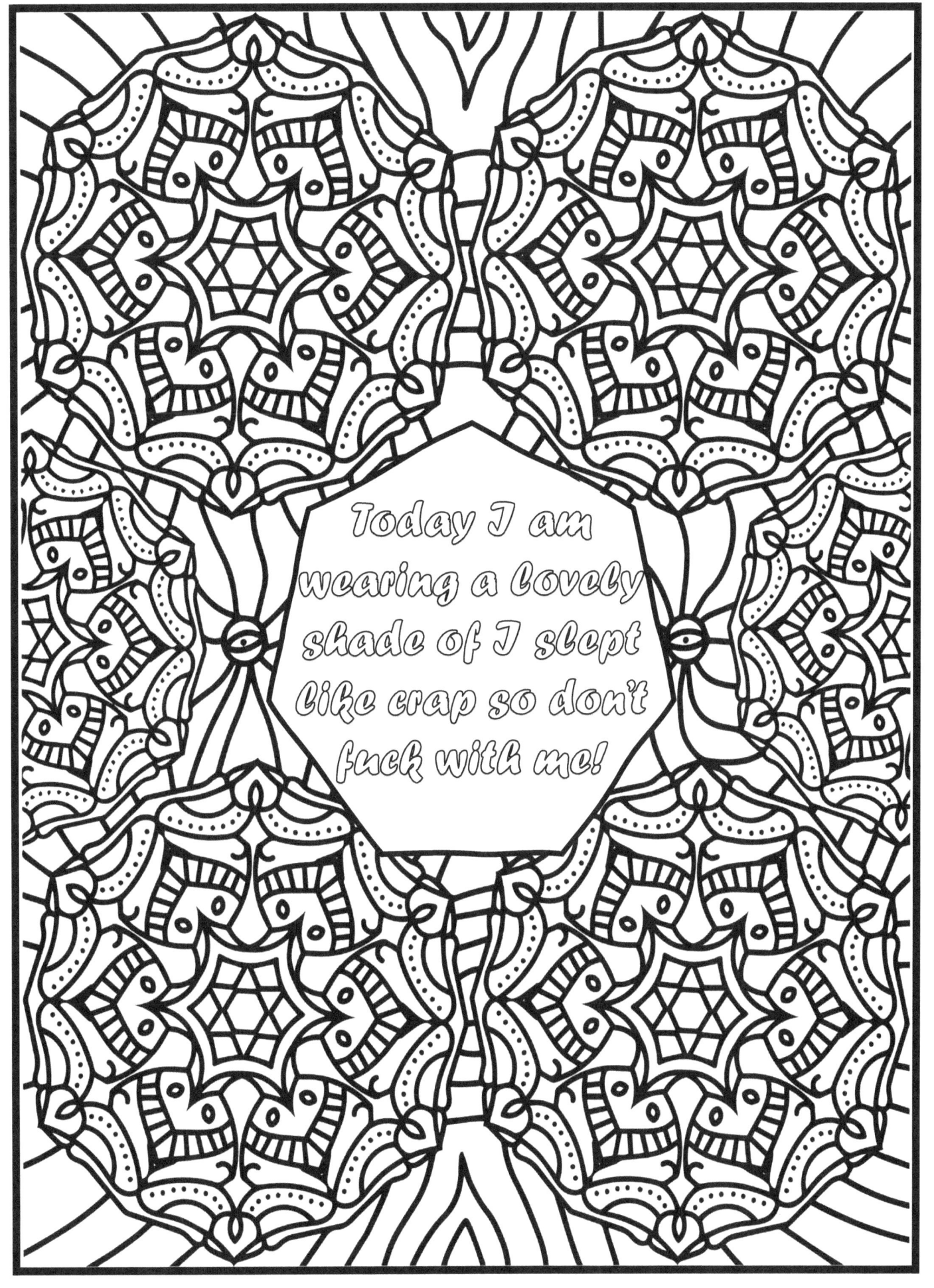

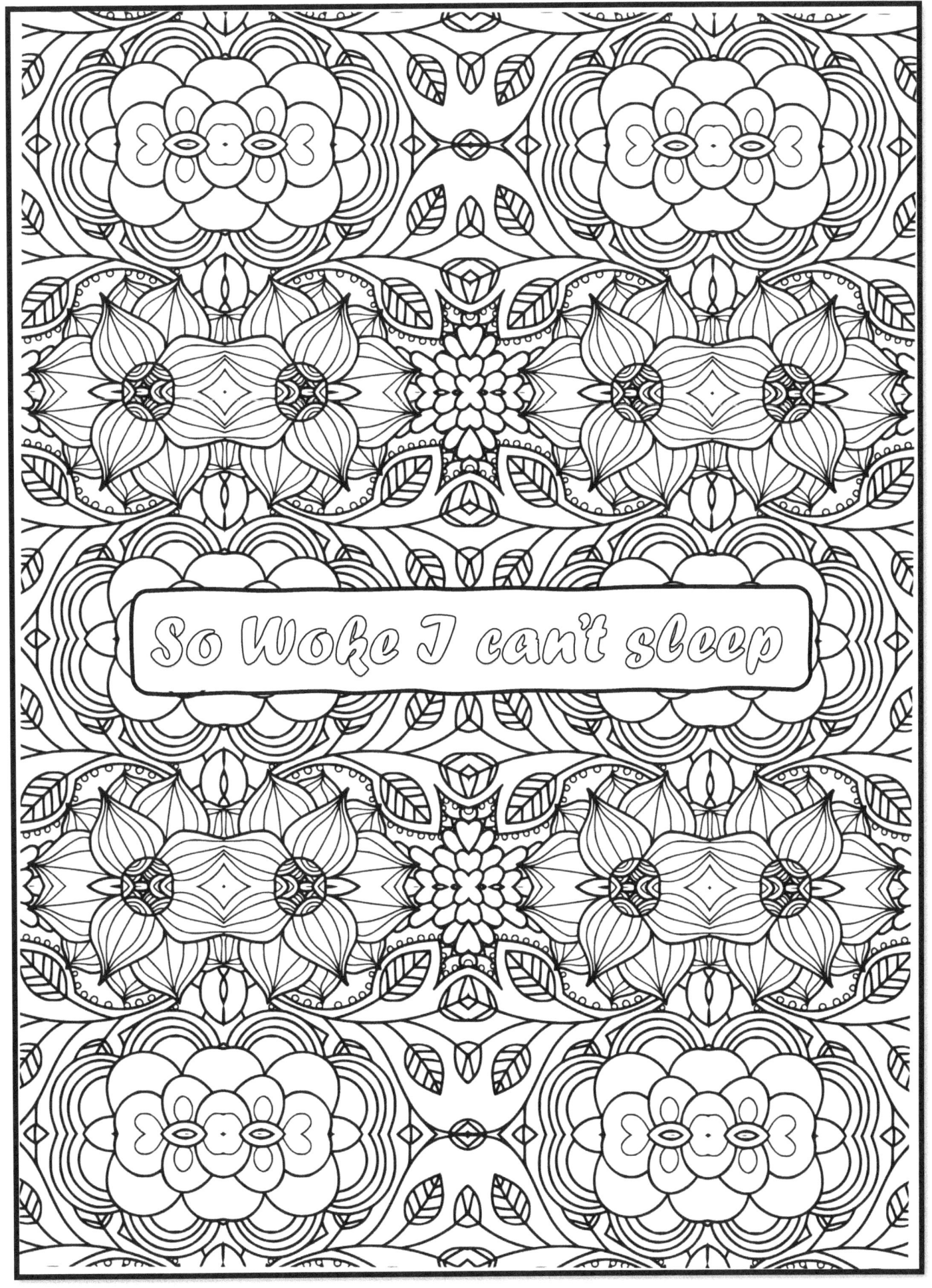

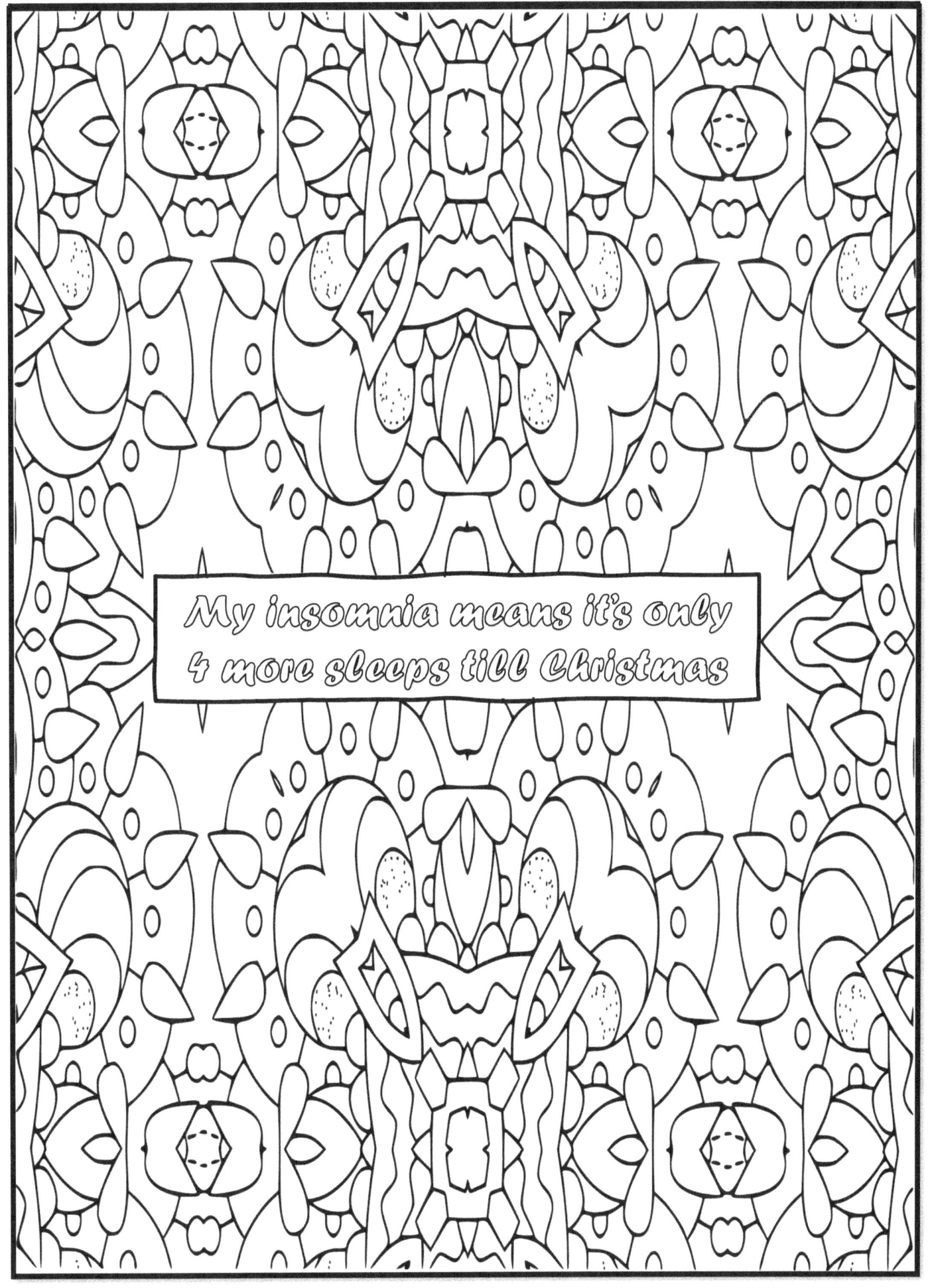

My insomnia means it's only 4 more sleeps till Christmas

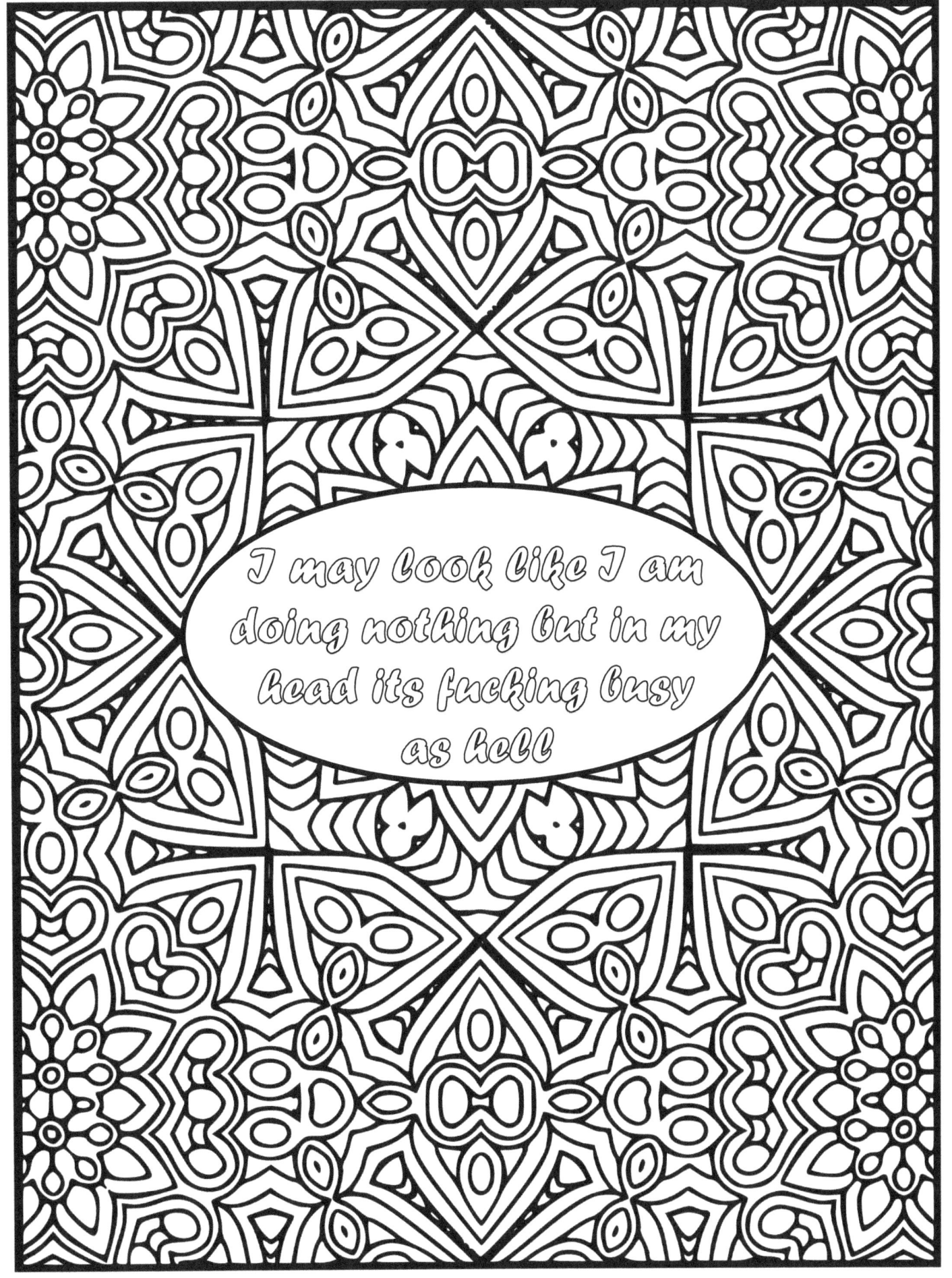

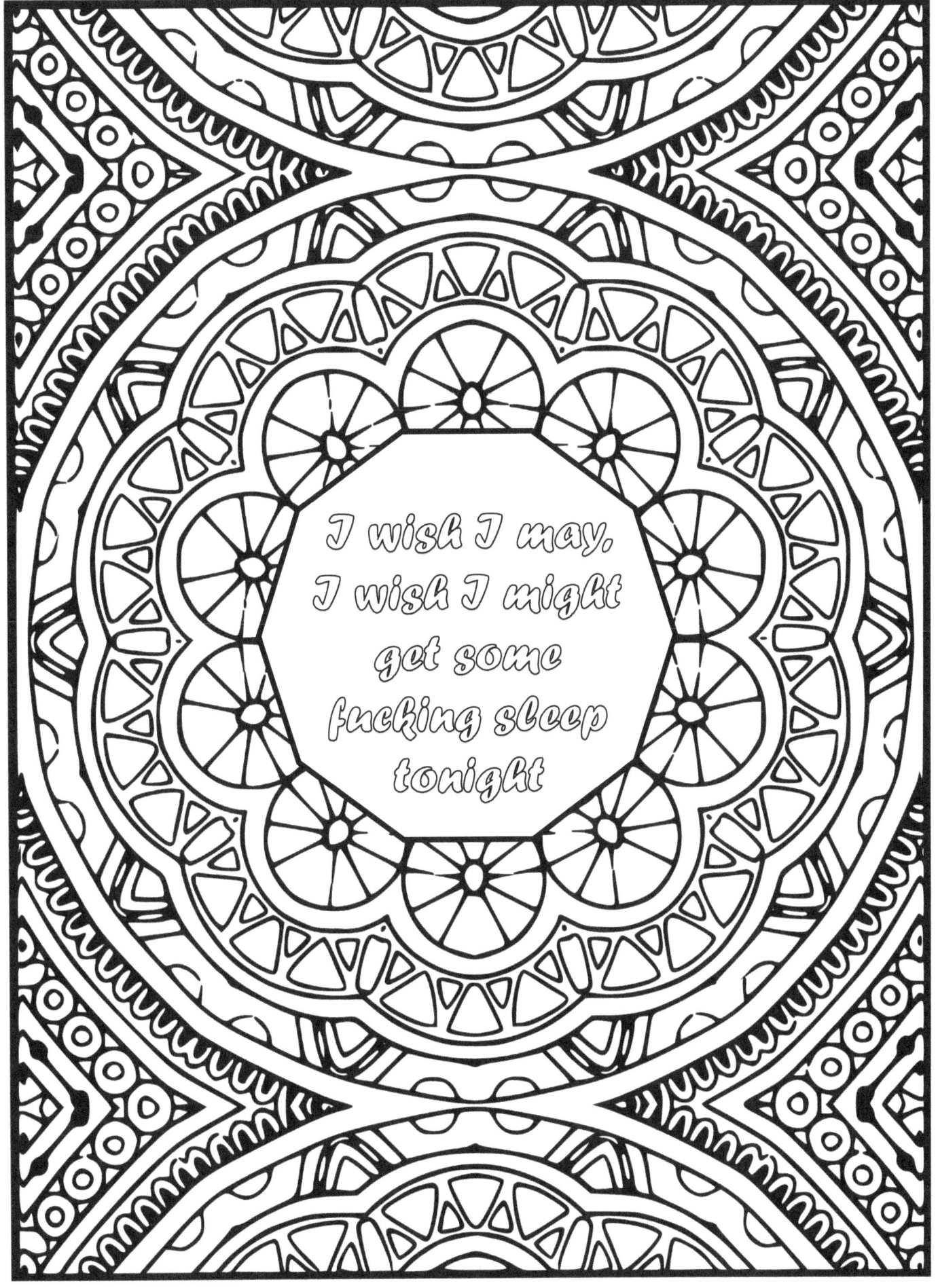

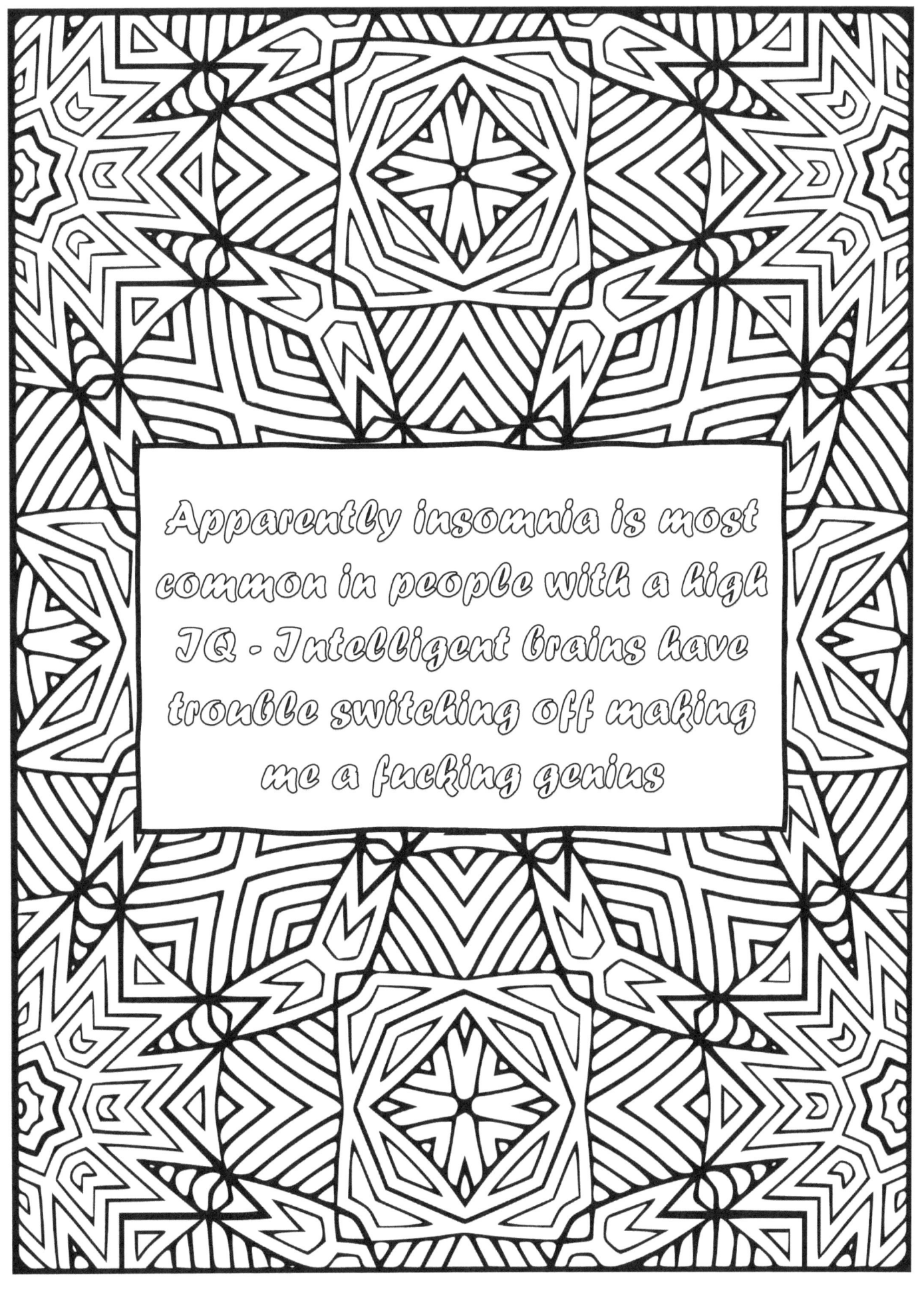

Apparently insomnia is most common in people with a high IQ - Intelligent brains have trouble switching off making me a fucking genius

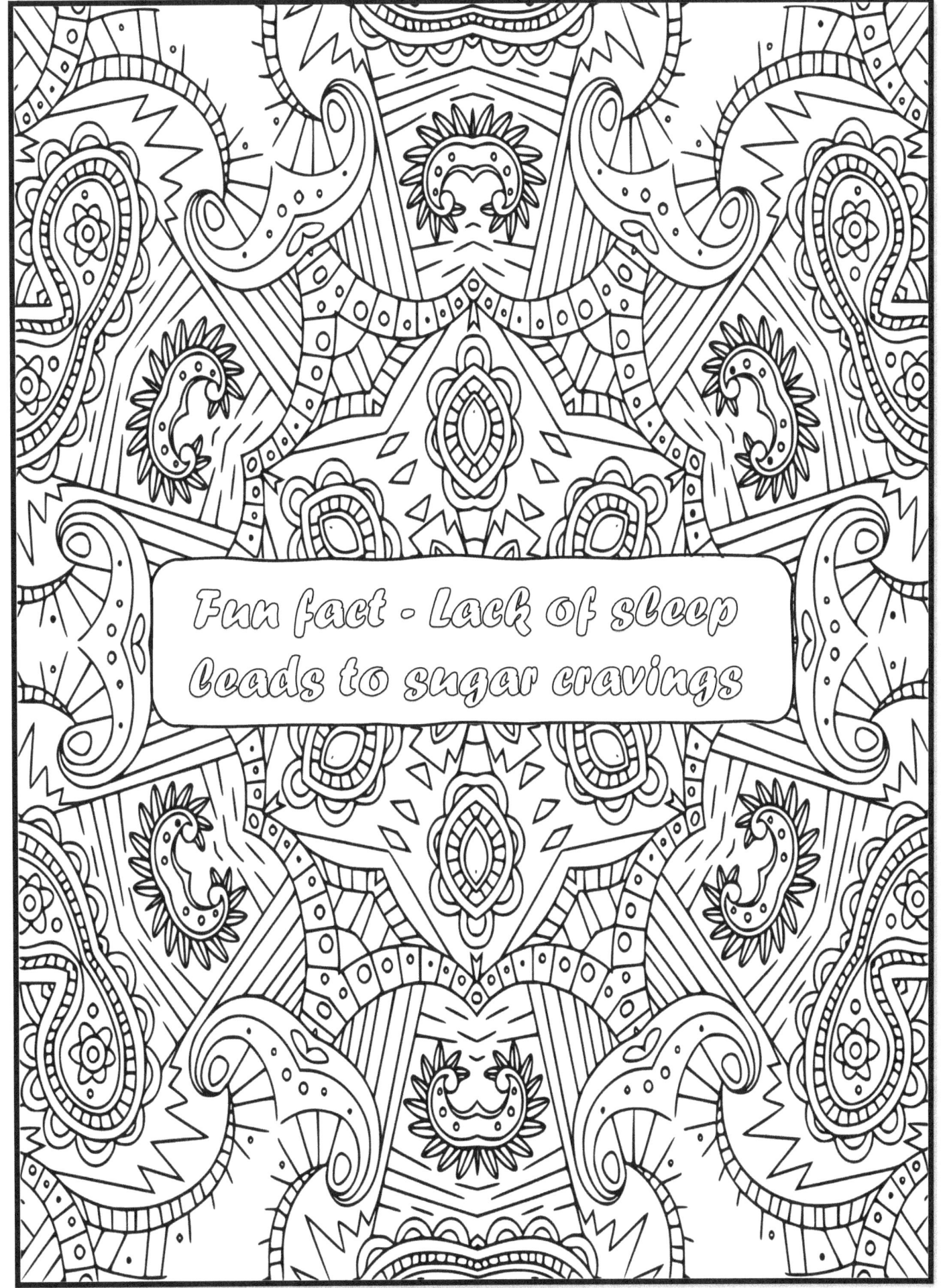

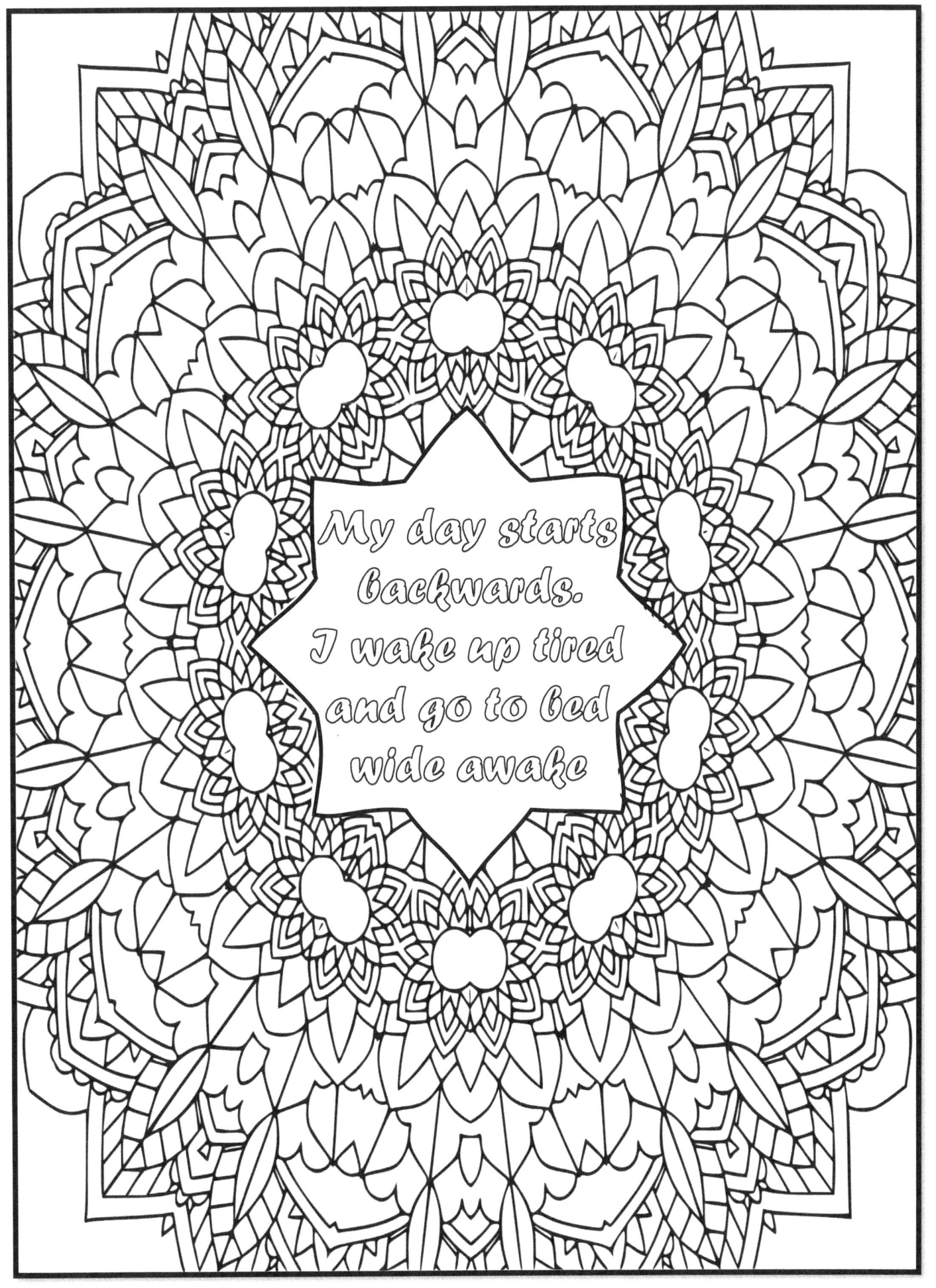

My day starts backwards. I wake up tired and go to bed wide awake

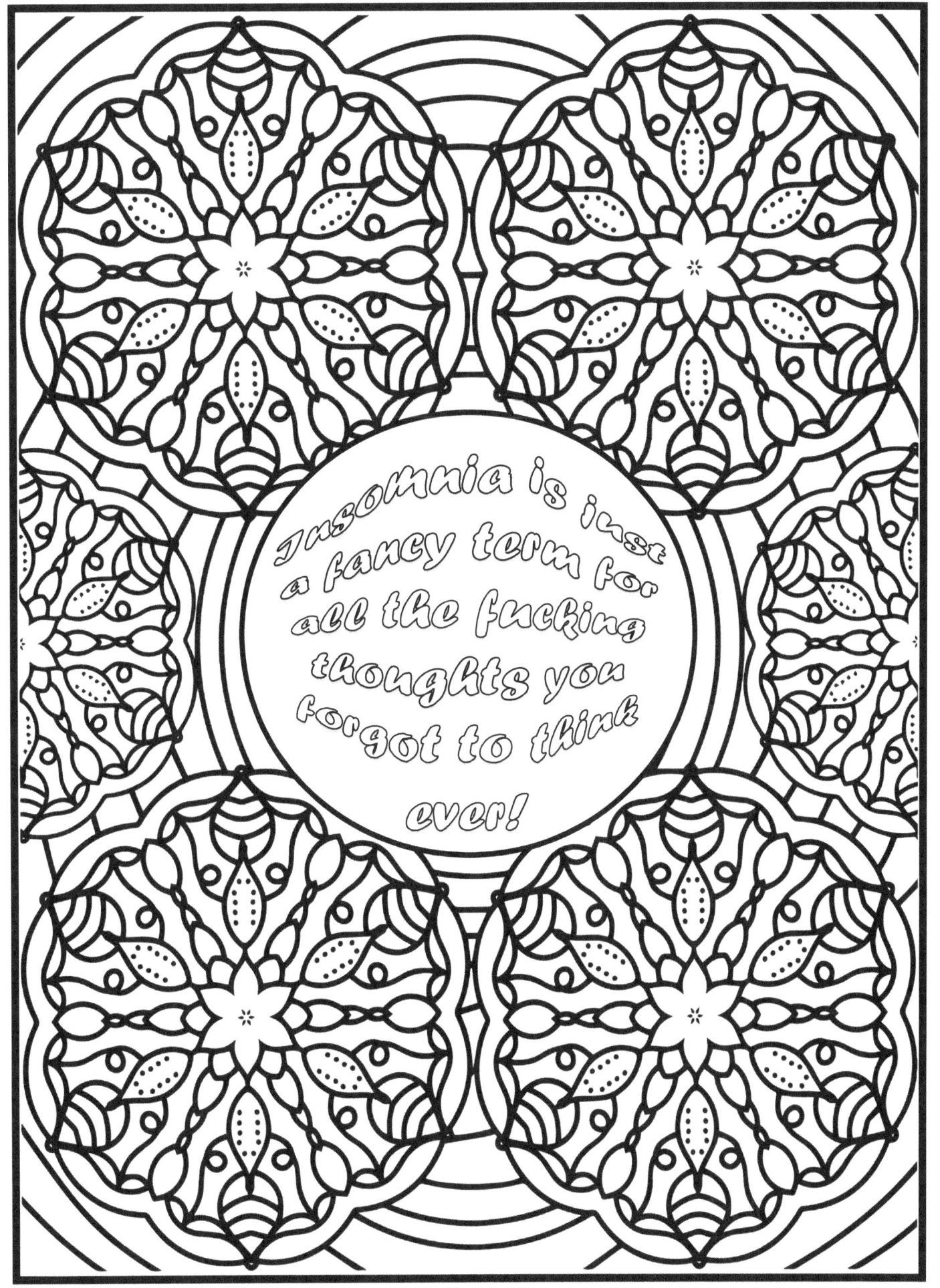

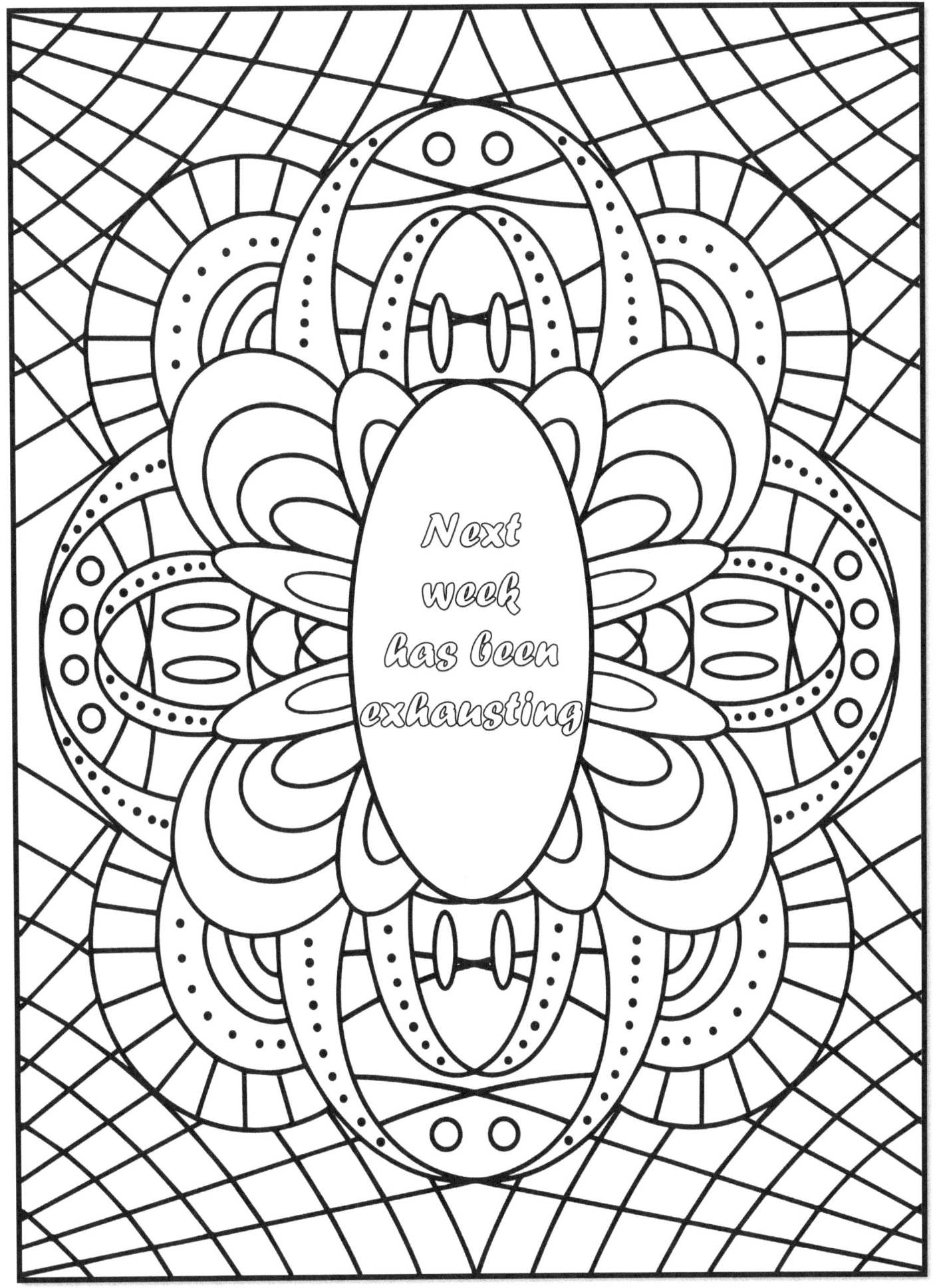

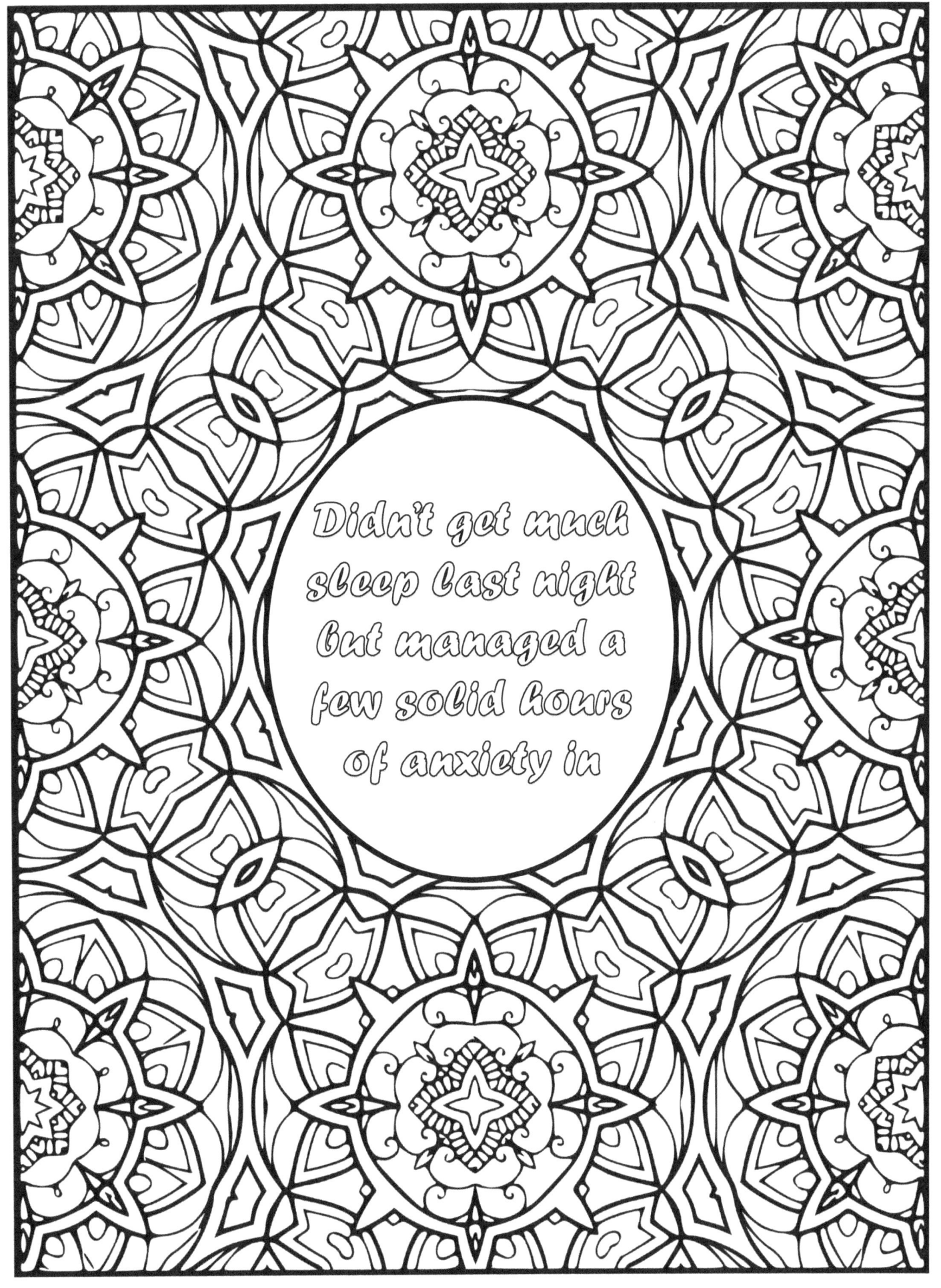

Didn't get much sleep last night but managed a few solid hours of anxiety in

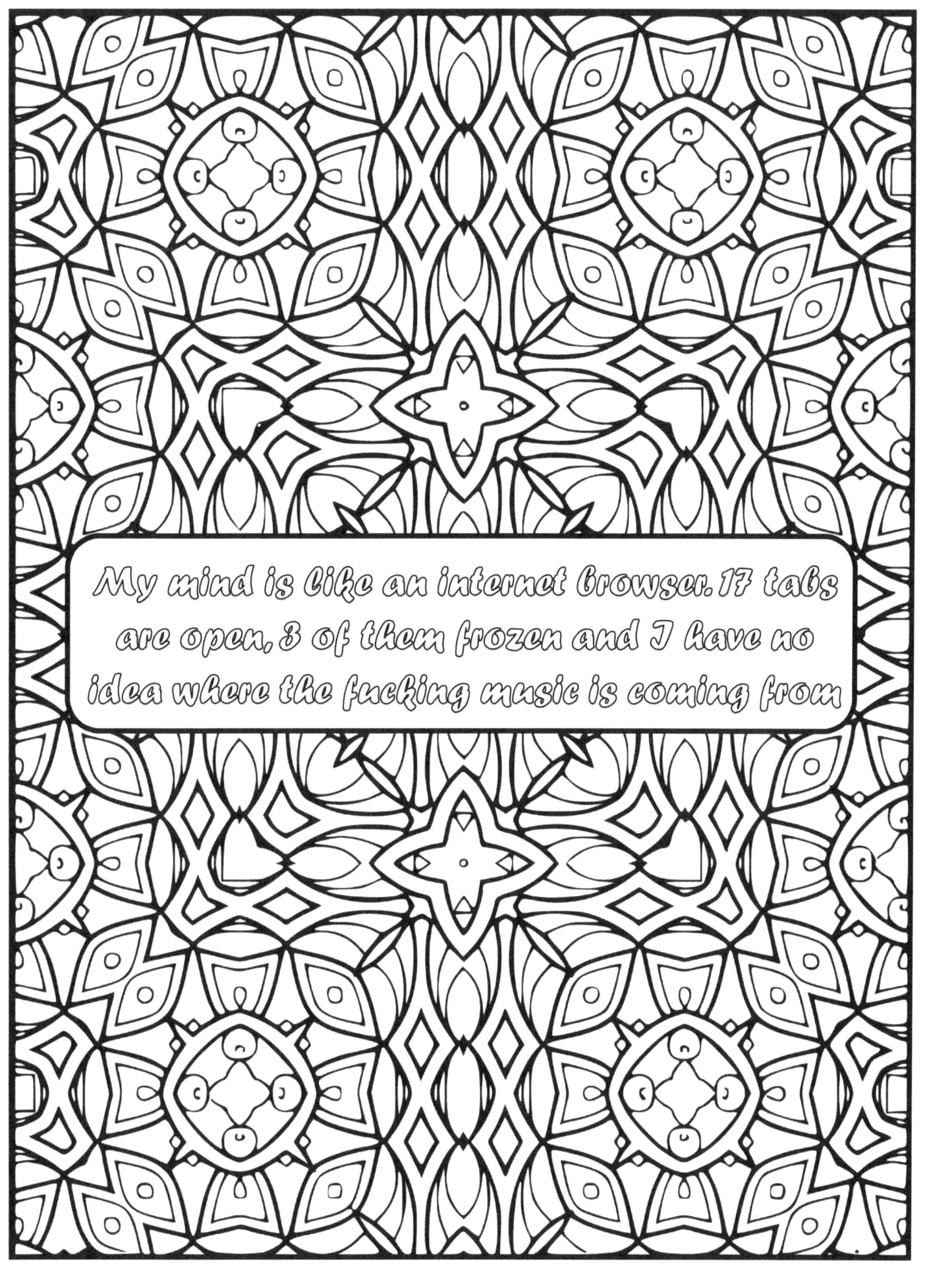

My mind is like an internet browser. 17 tabs are open, 3 of them frozen and I have no idea where the fucking music is coming from

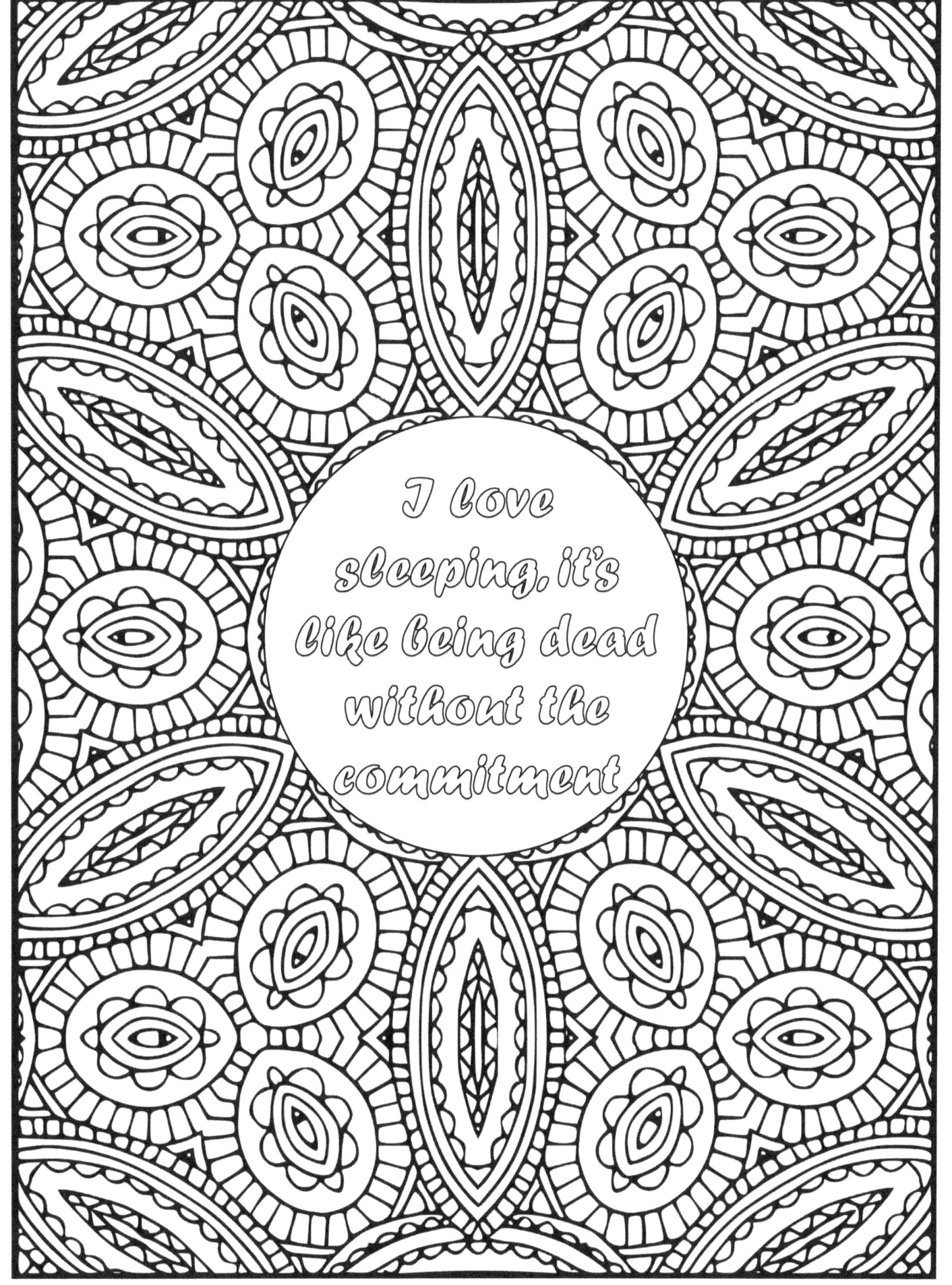

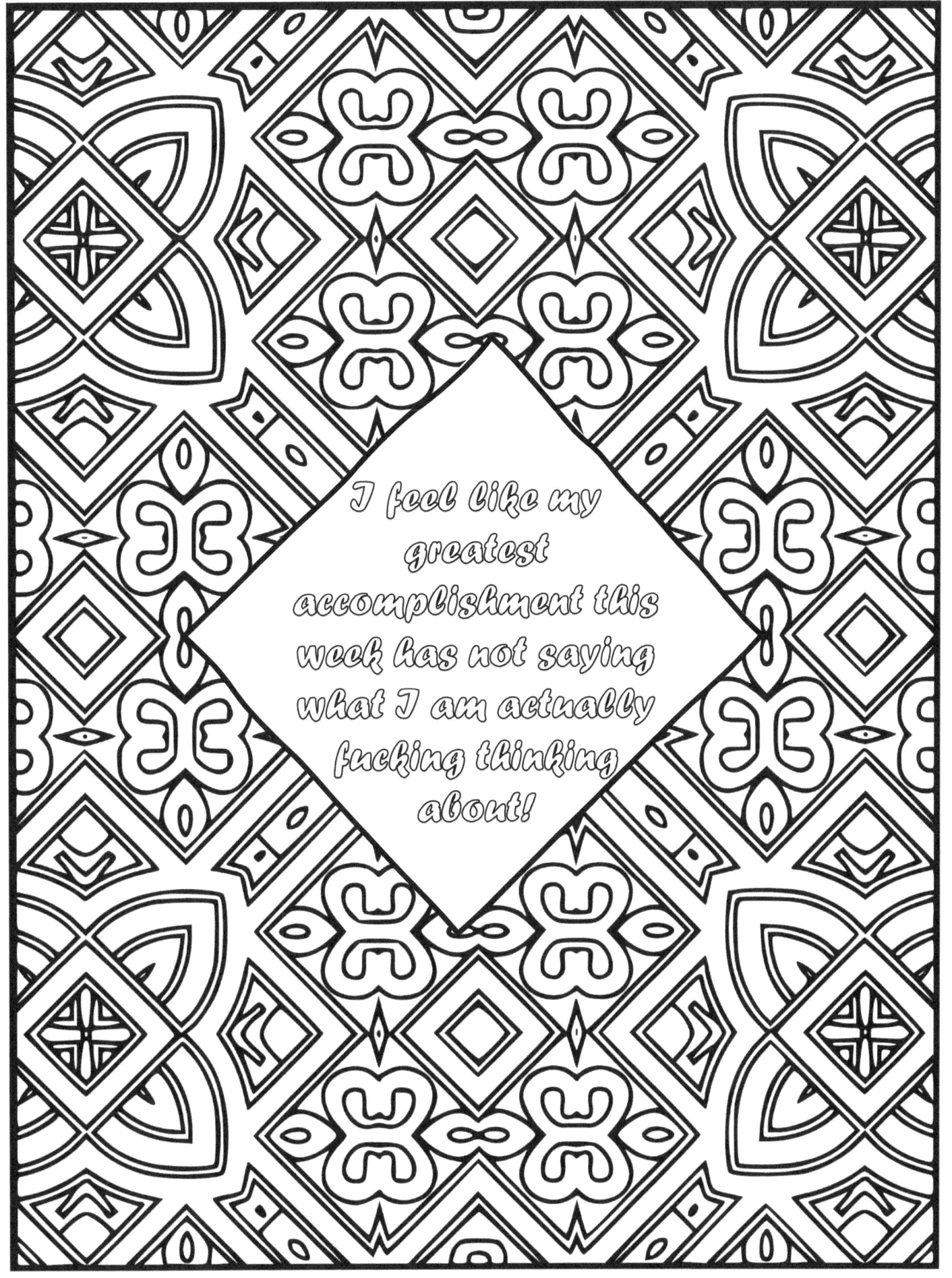

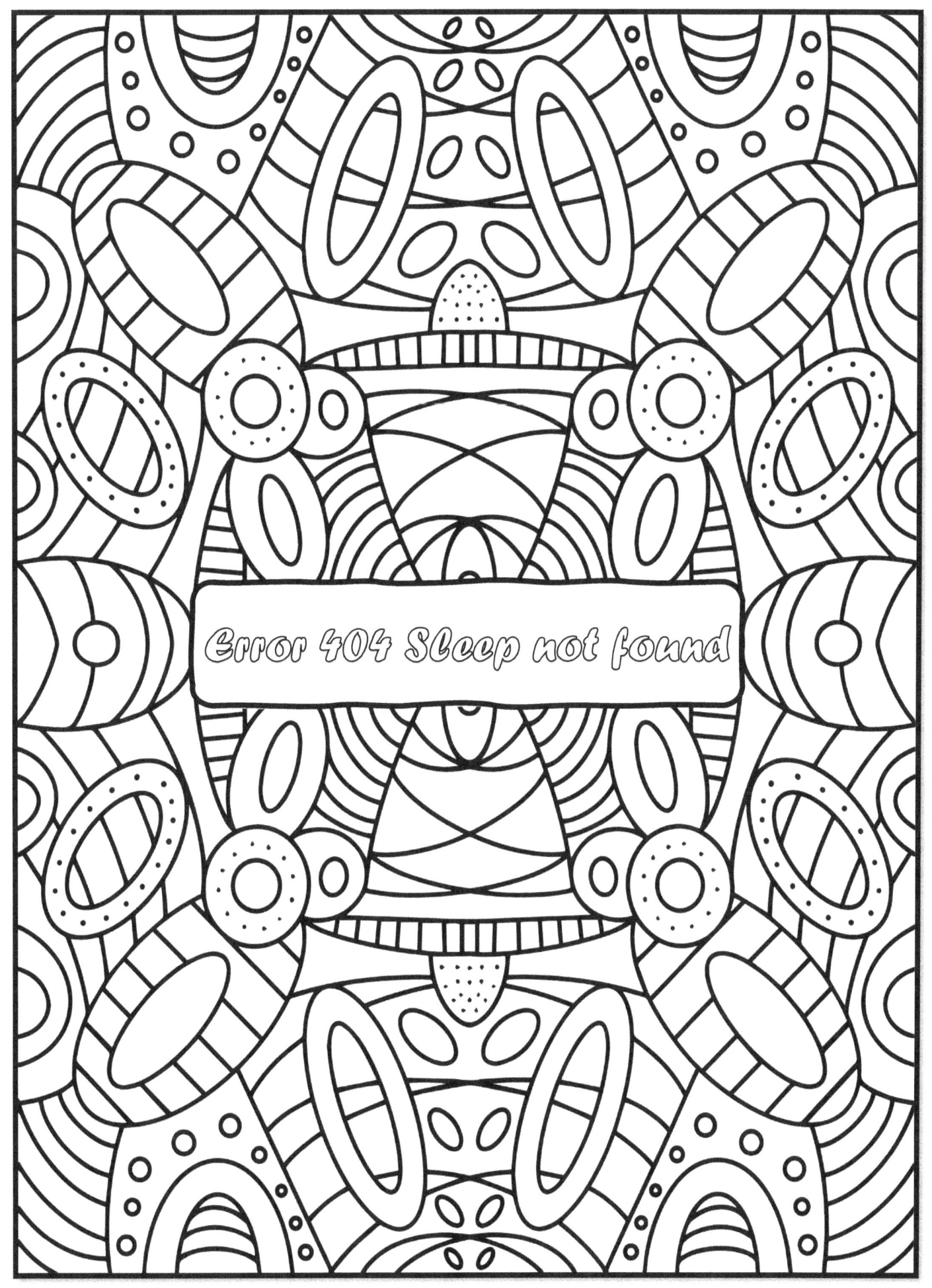

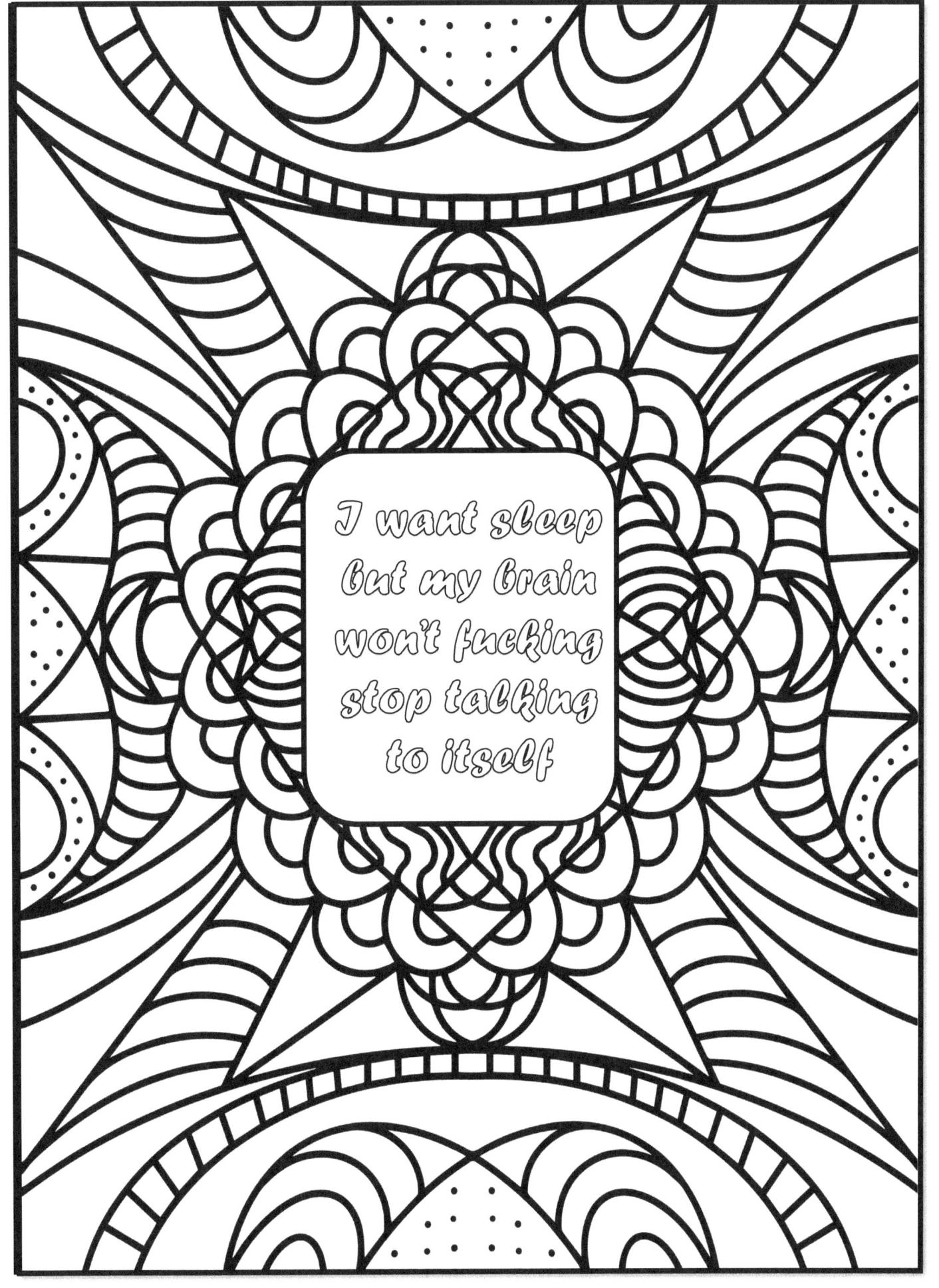

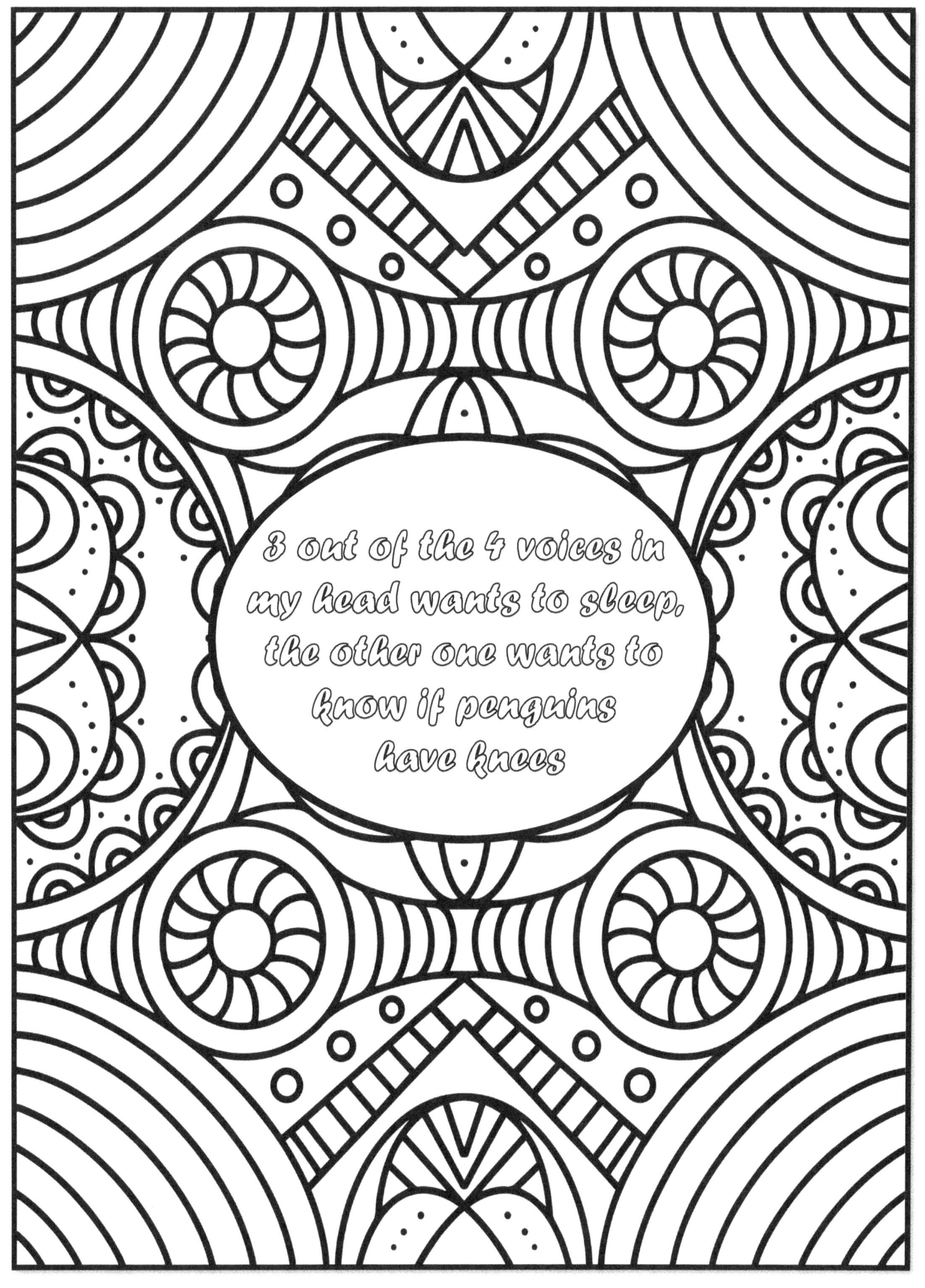

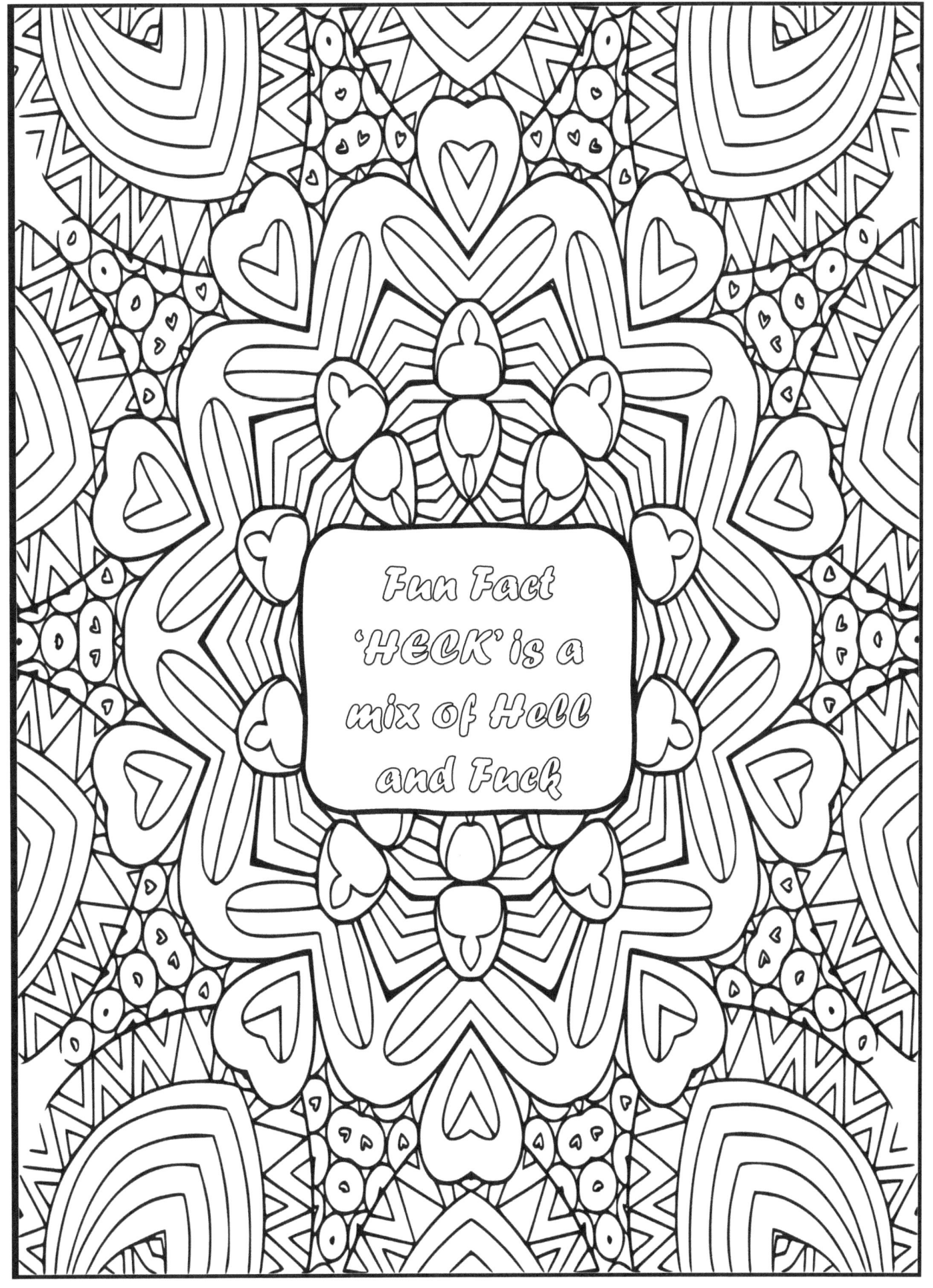

Fun Fact 'HECK' is a mix of Hell and Fuck

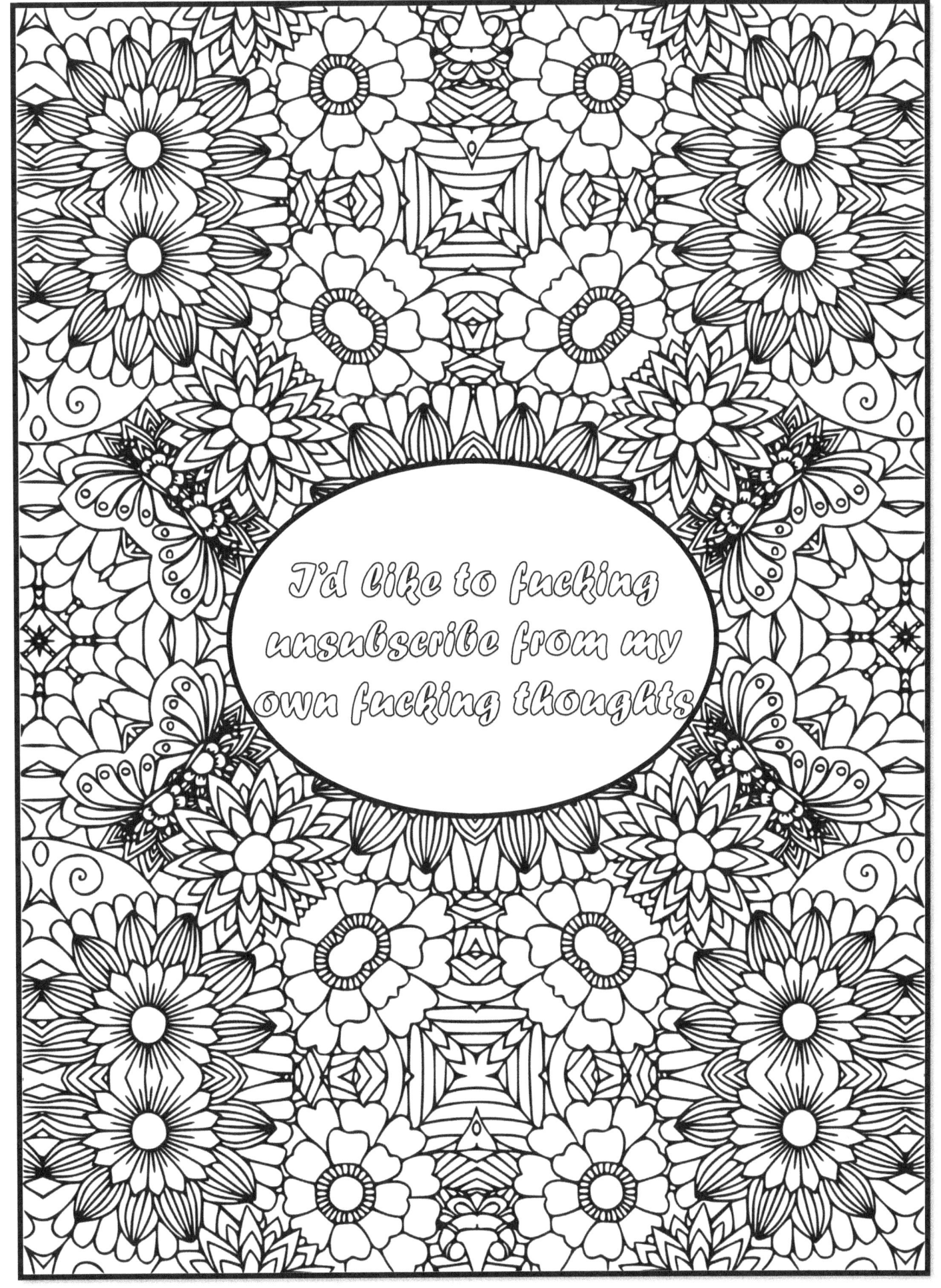

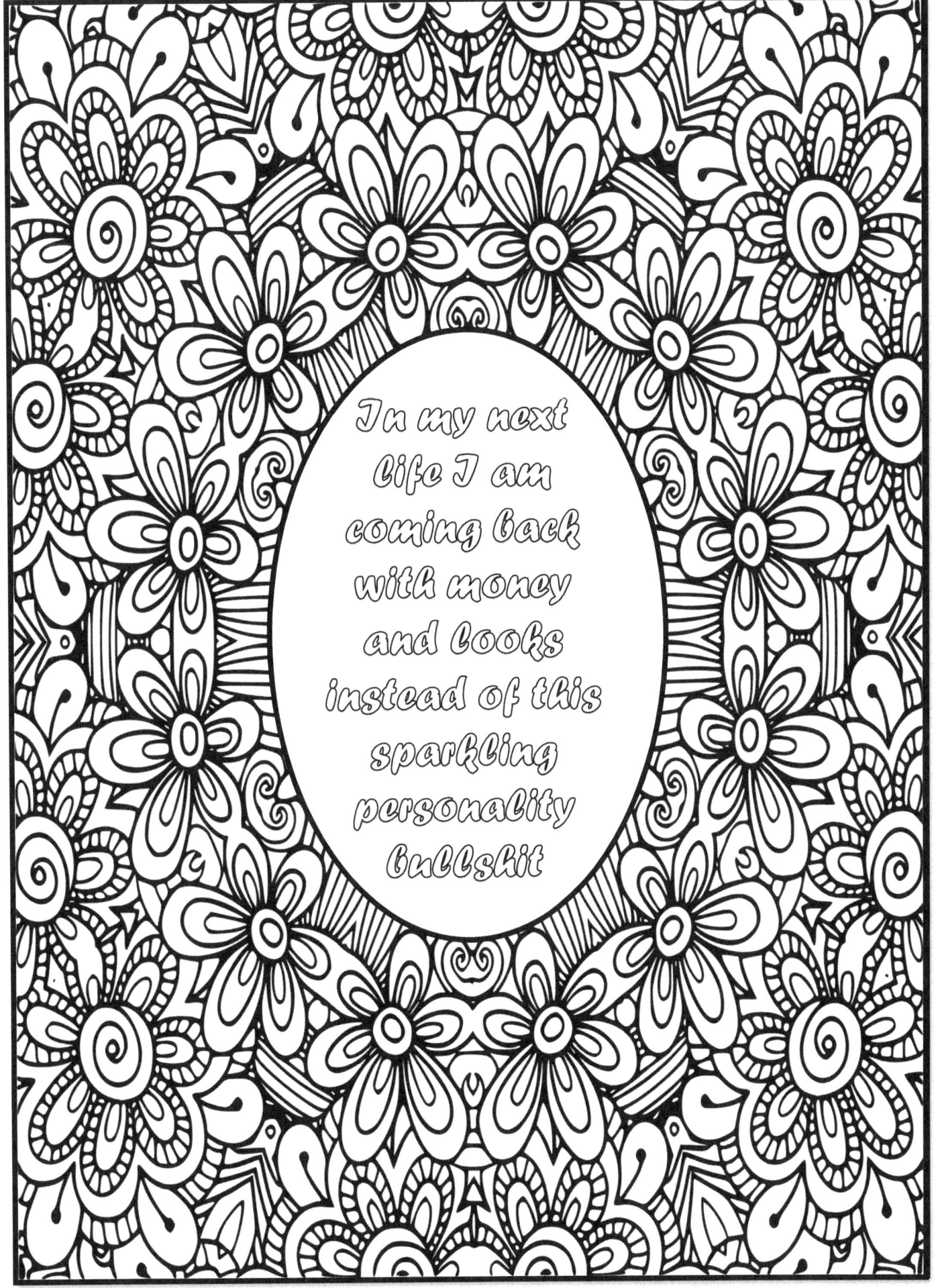

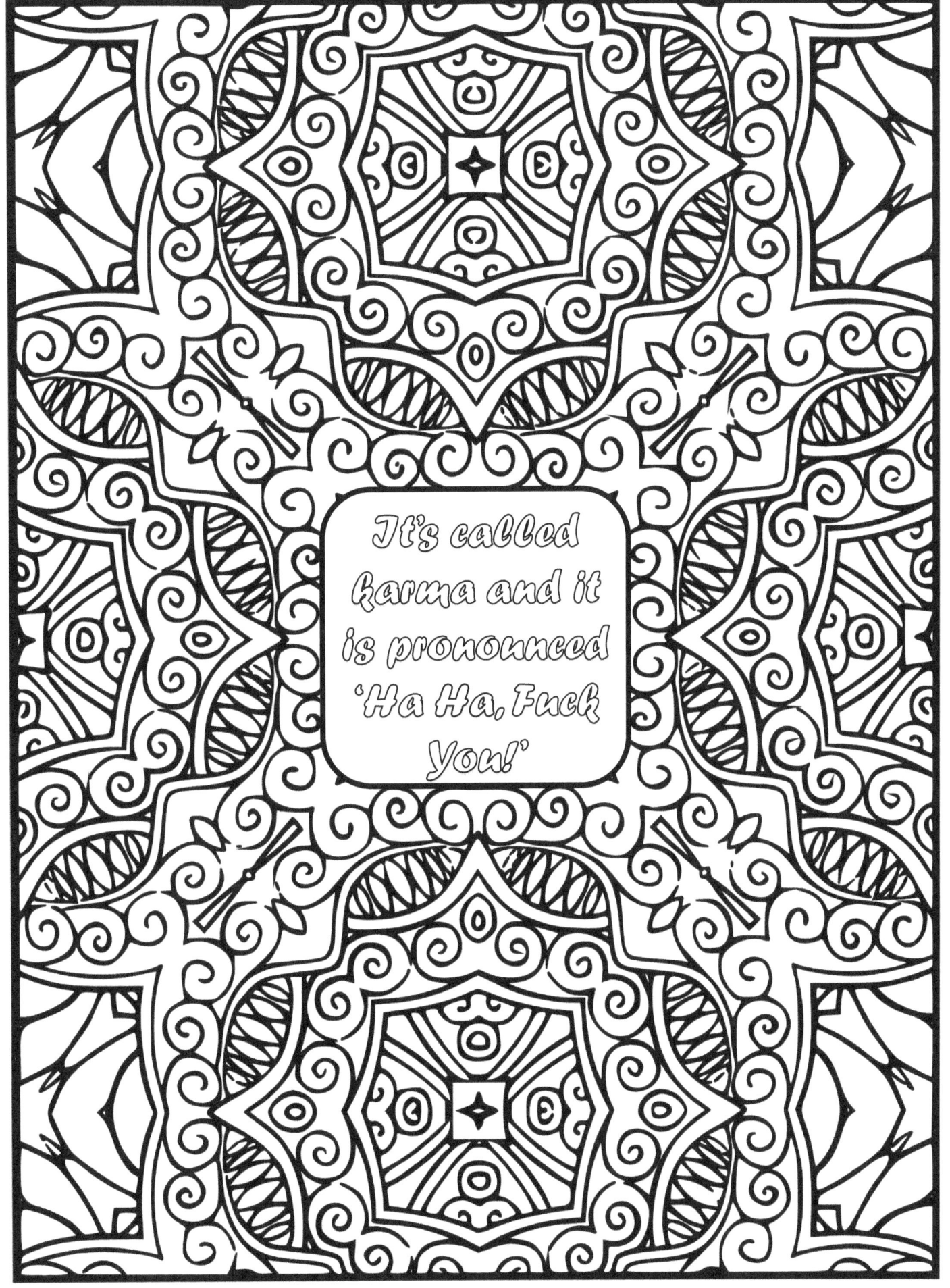

It's called karma and it is pronounced 'Ha Ha, Fuck You!'

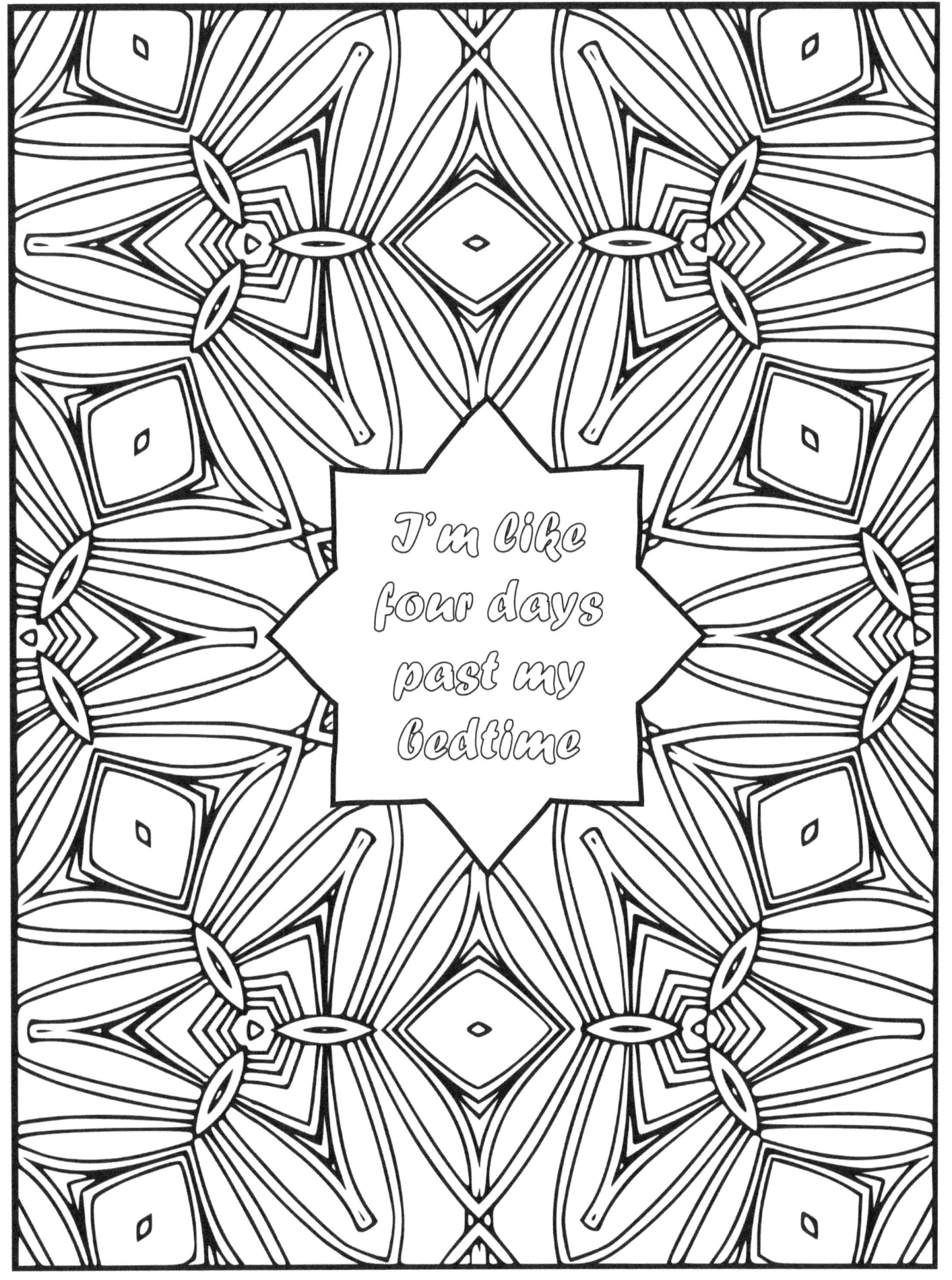

I'm like four days past my bedtime

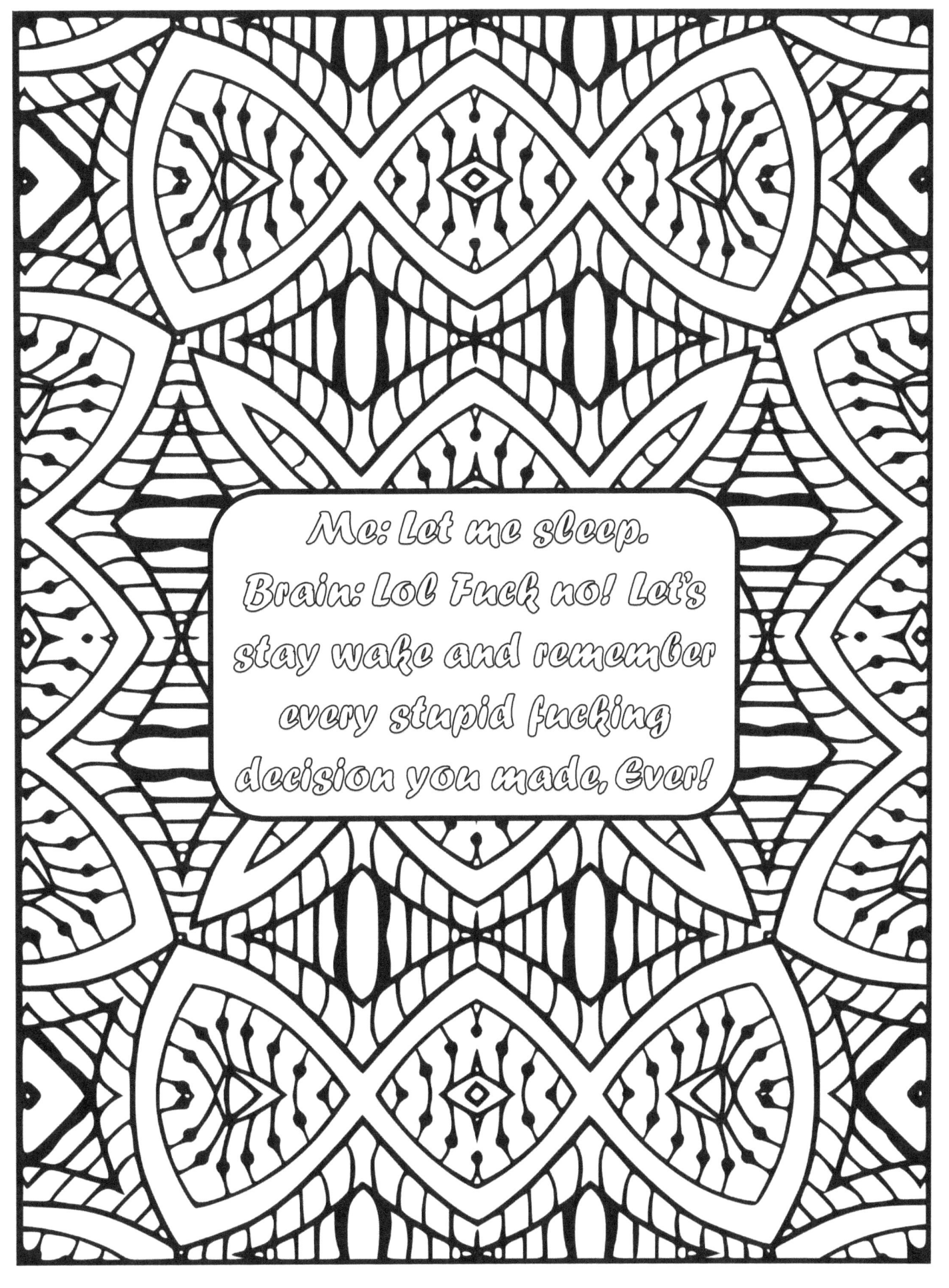

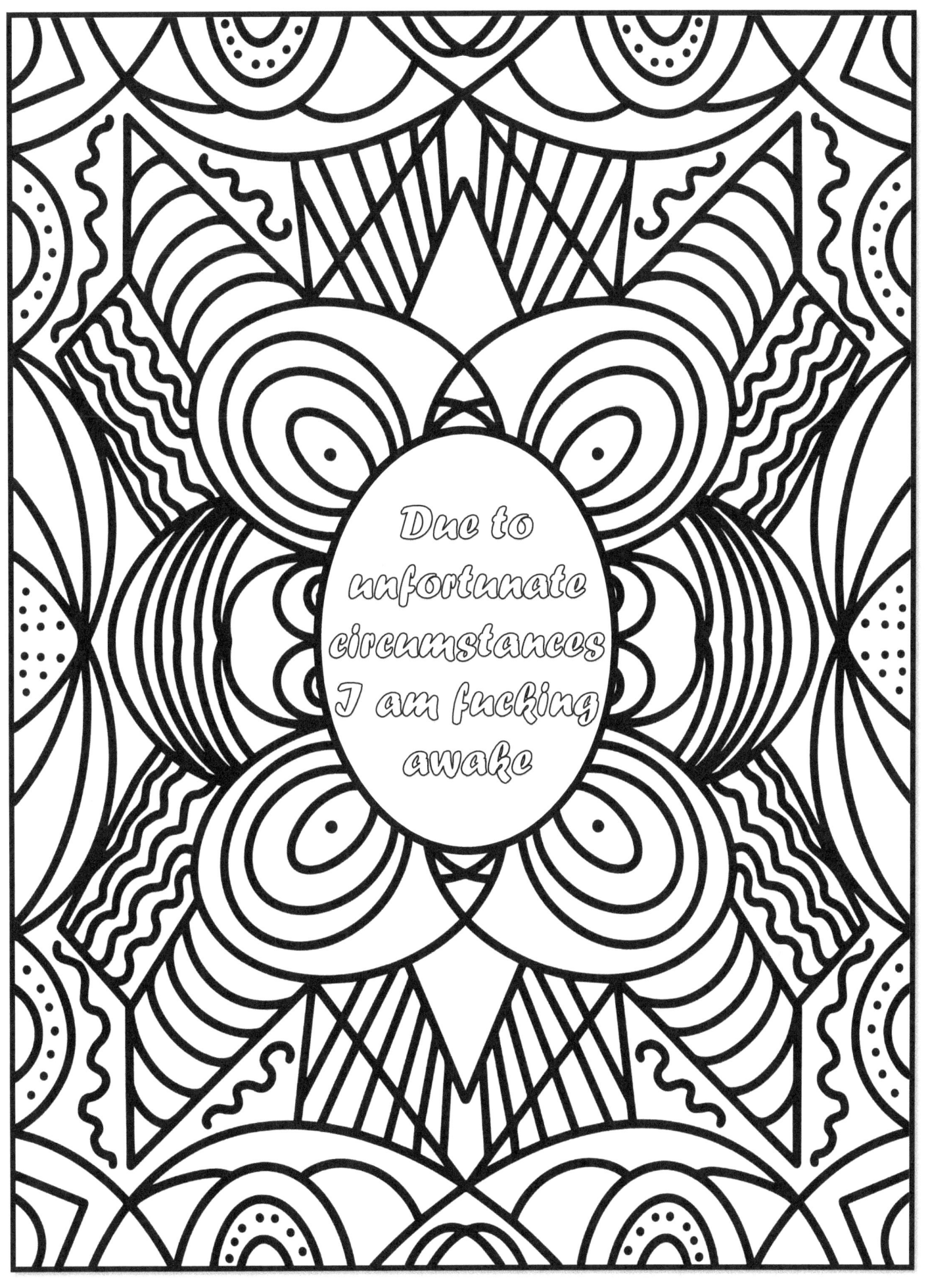

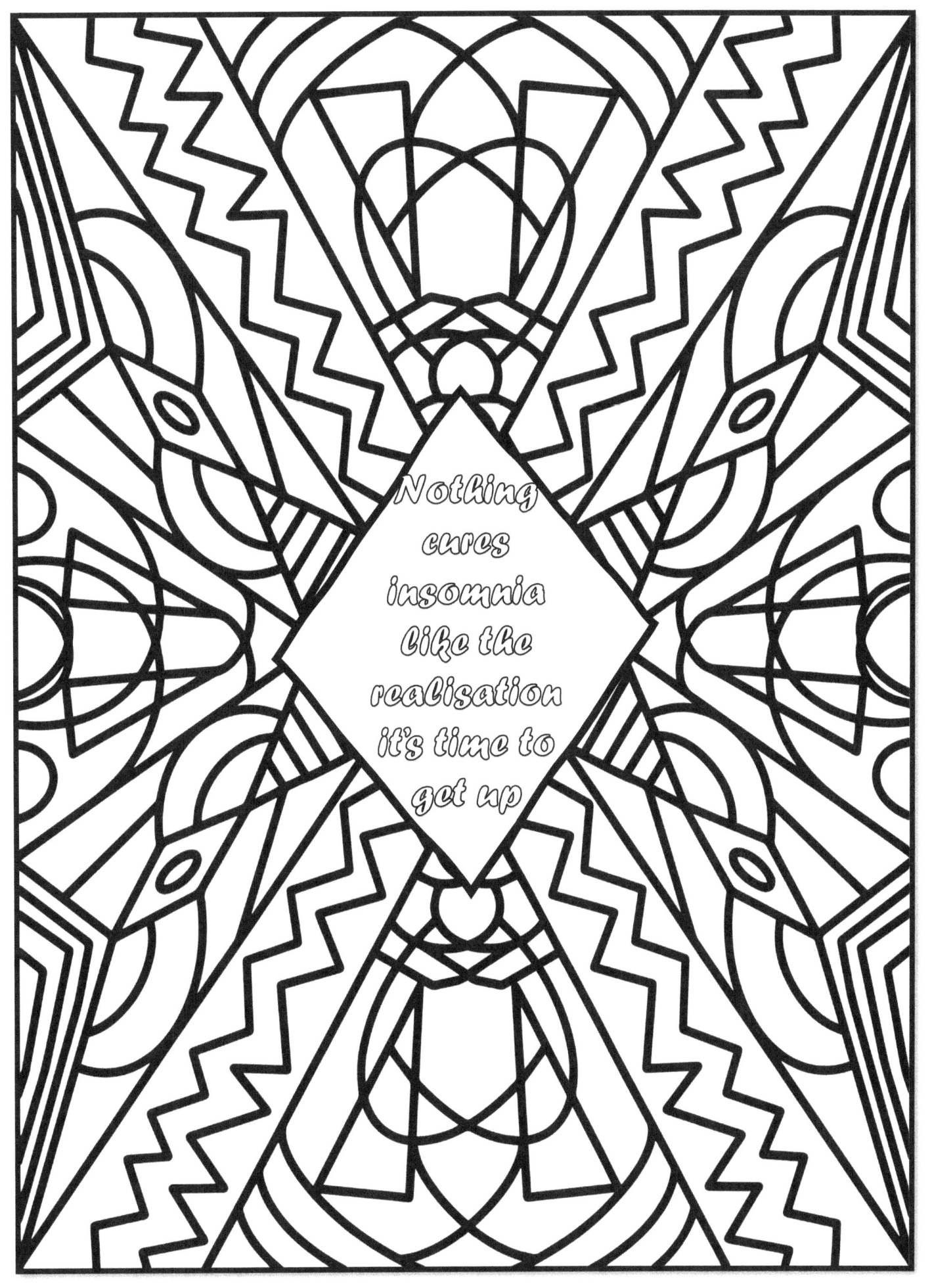

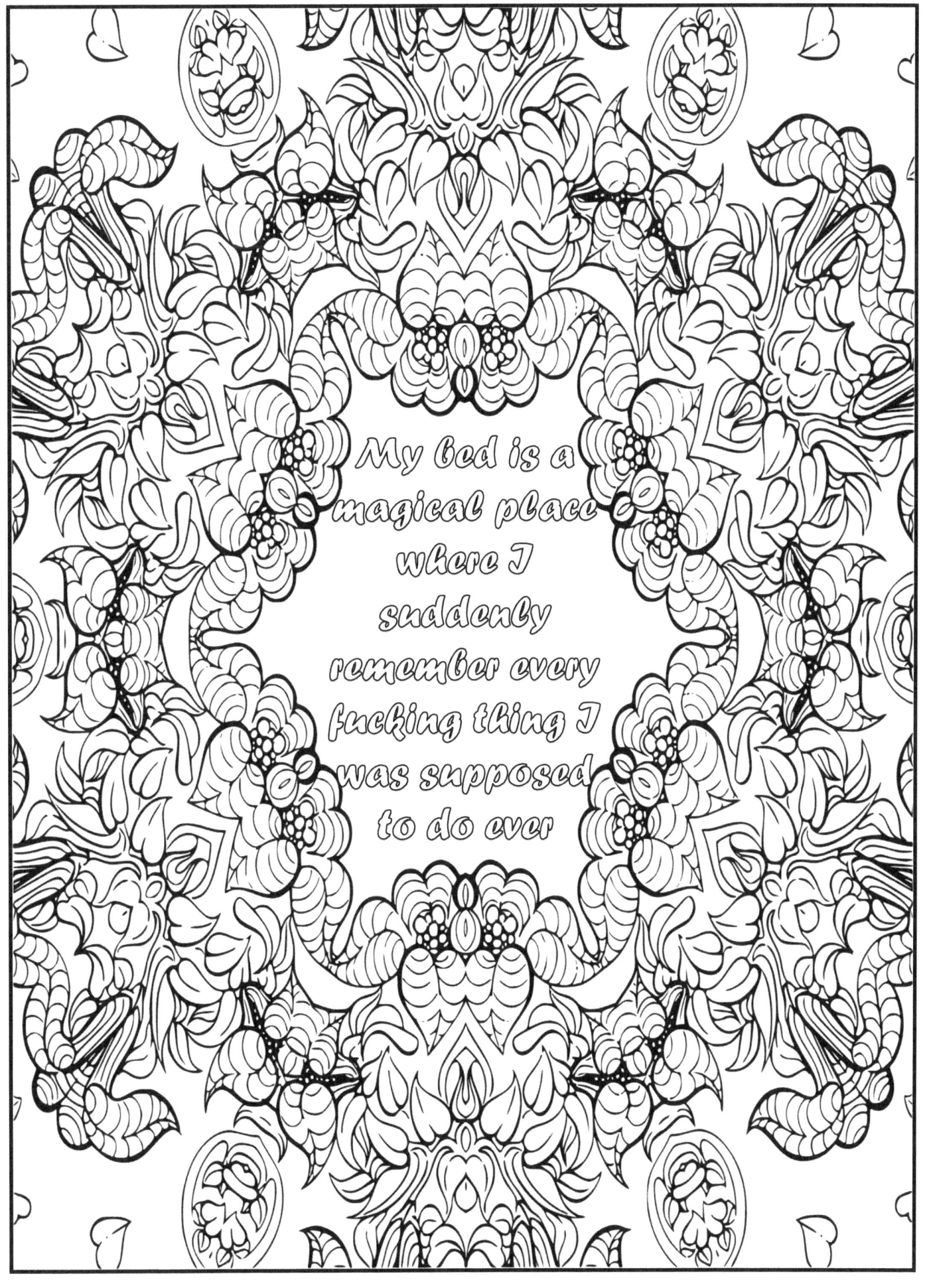

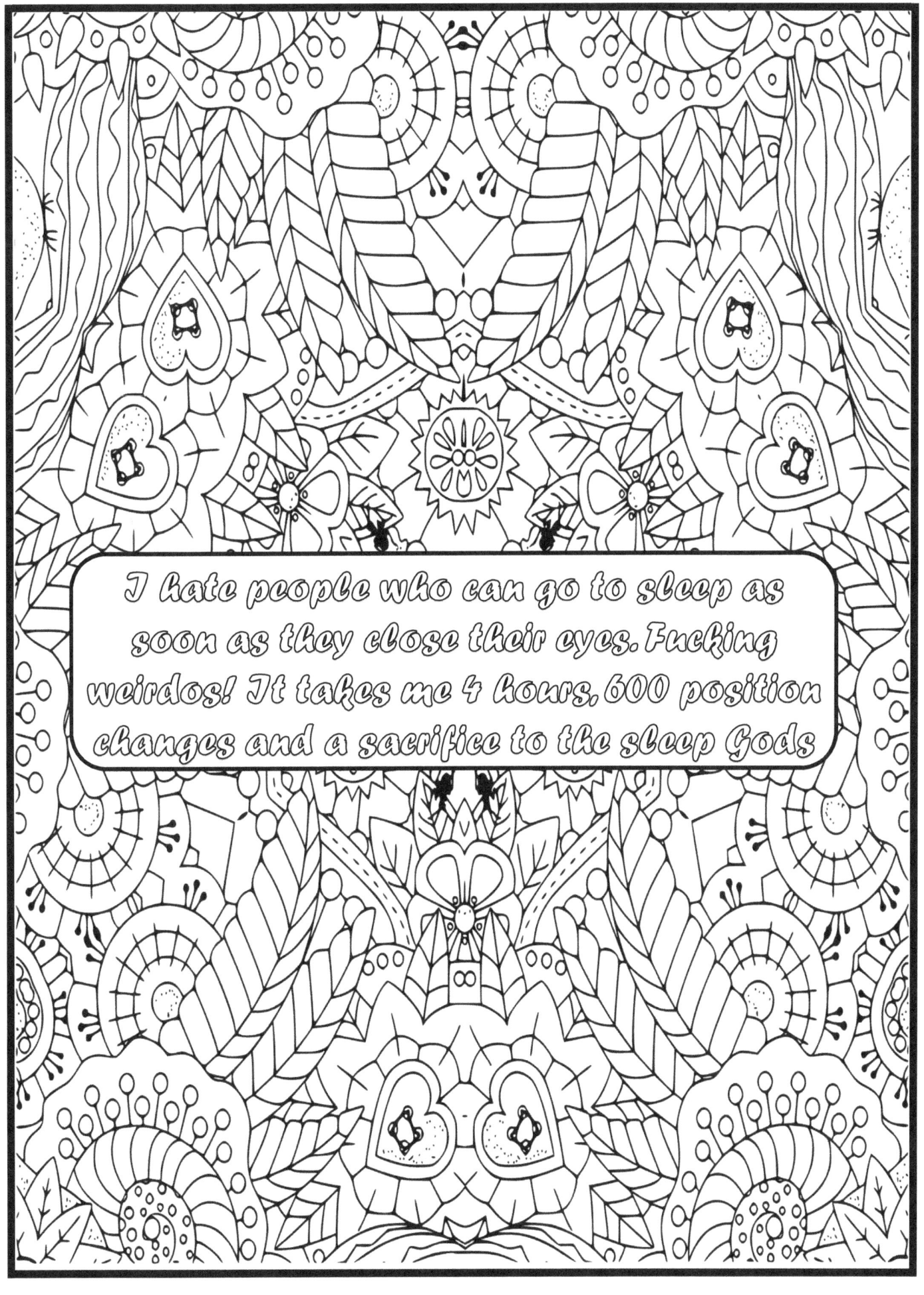

I hate people who can go to sleep as soon as they close their eyes. Fucking weirdos! It takes me 4 hours, 600 position changes and a sacrifice to the sleep Gods

I'm like 140% tired

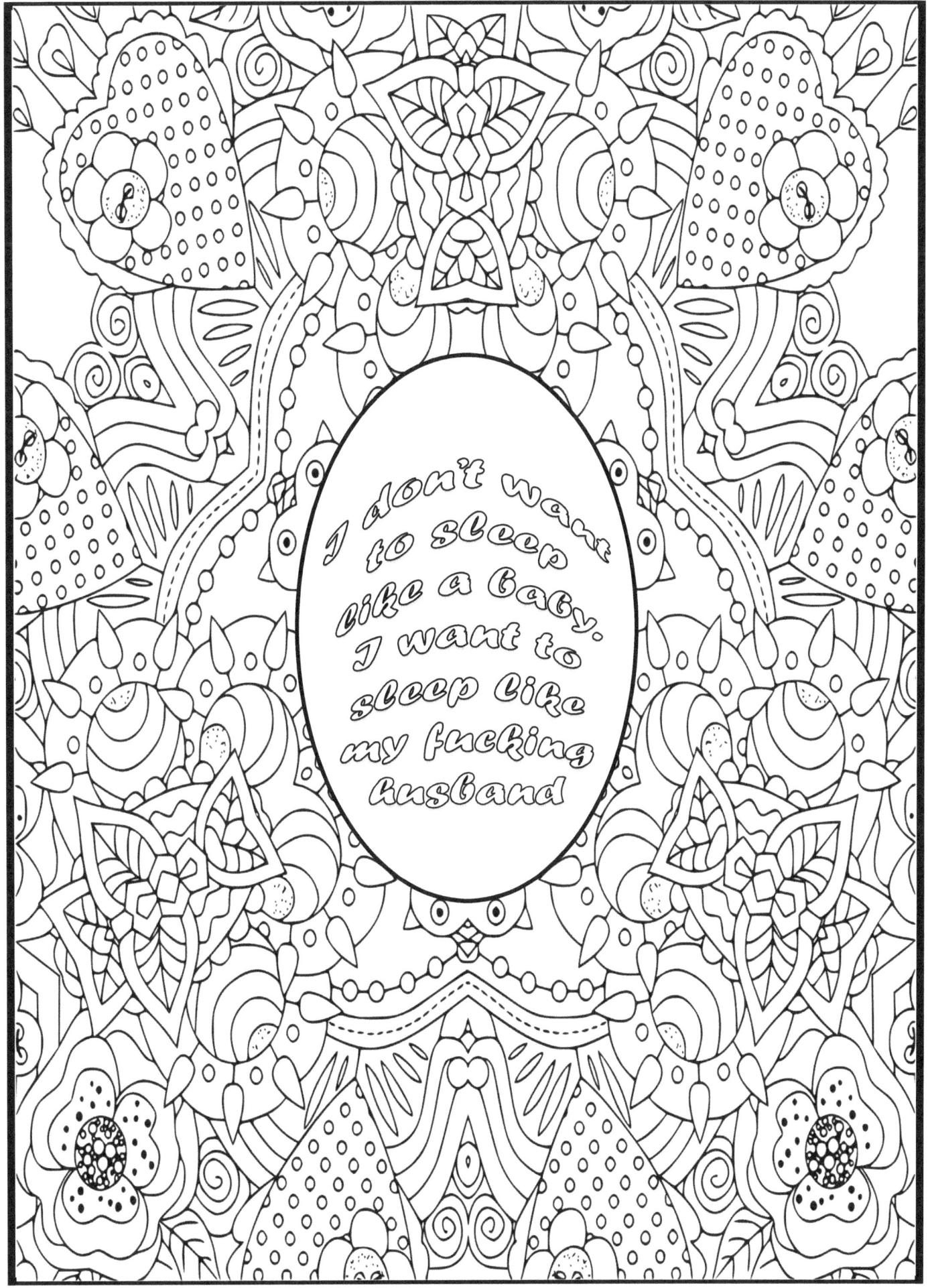

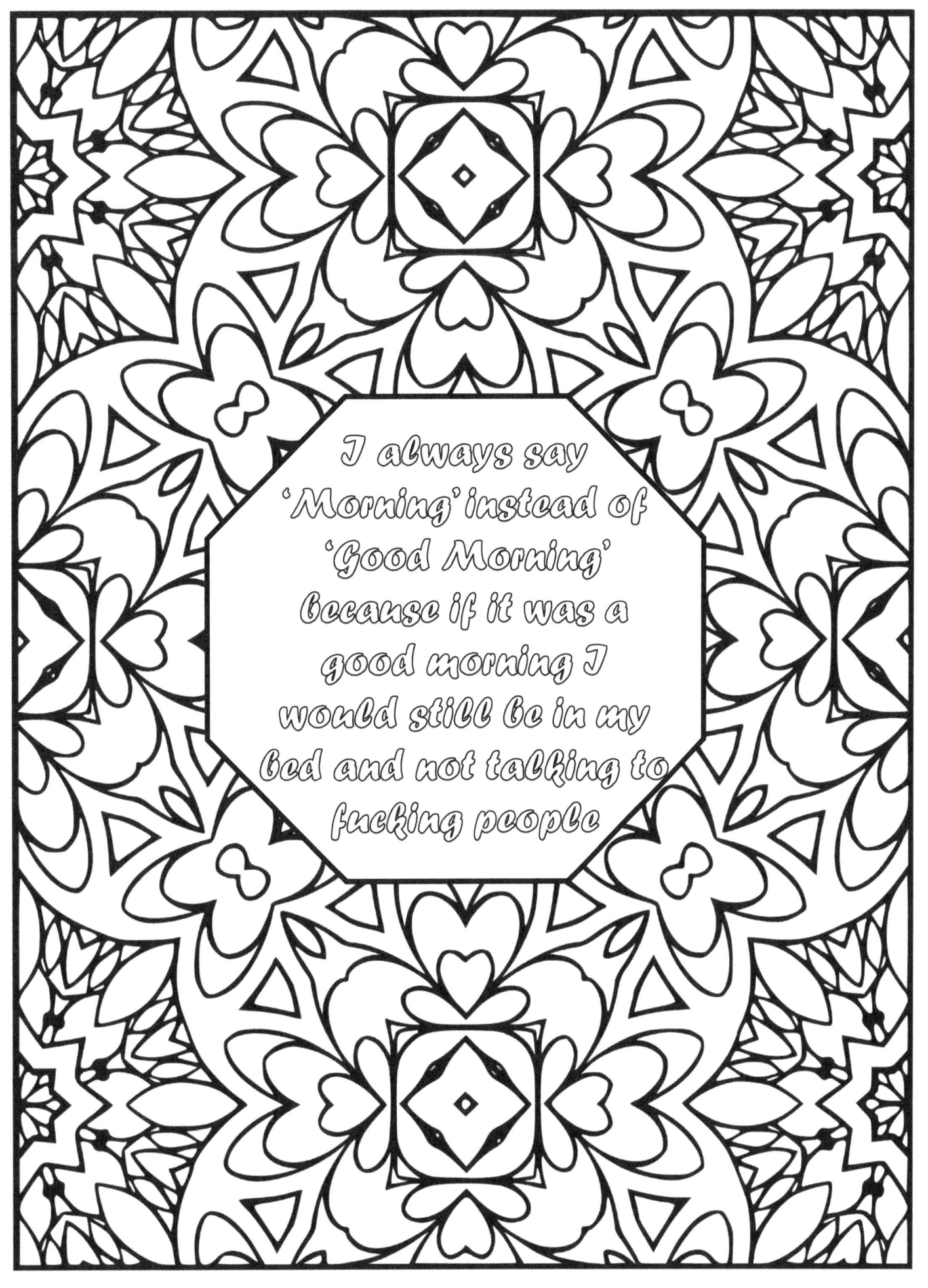

I always say 'Morning' instead of 'Good Morning' because if it was a good morning I would still be in my bed and not talking to fucking people

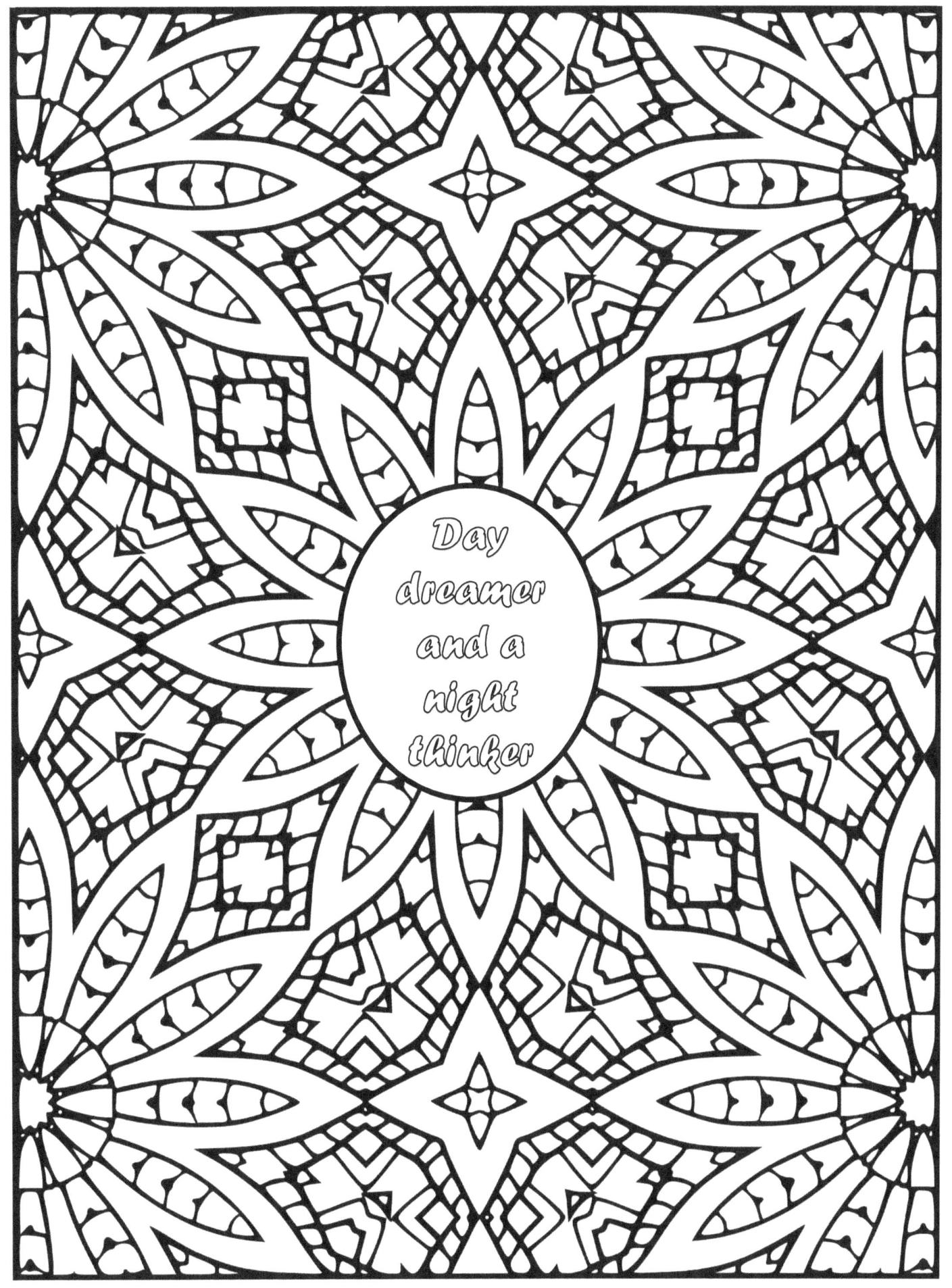

Day dreamer and a night thinker

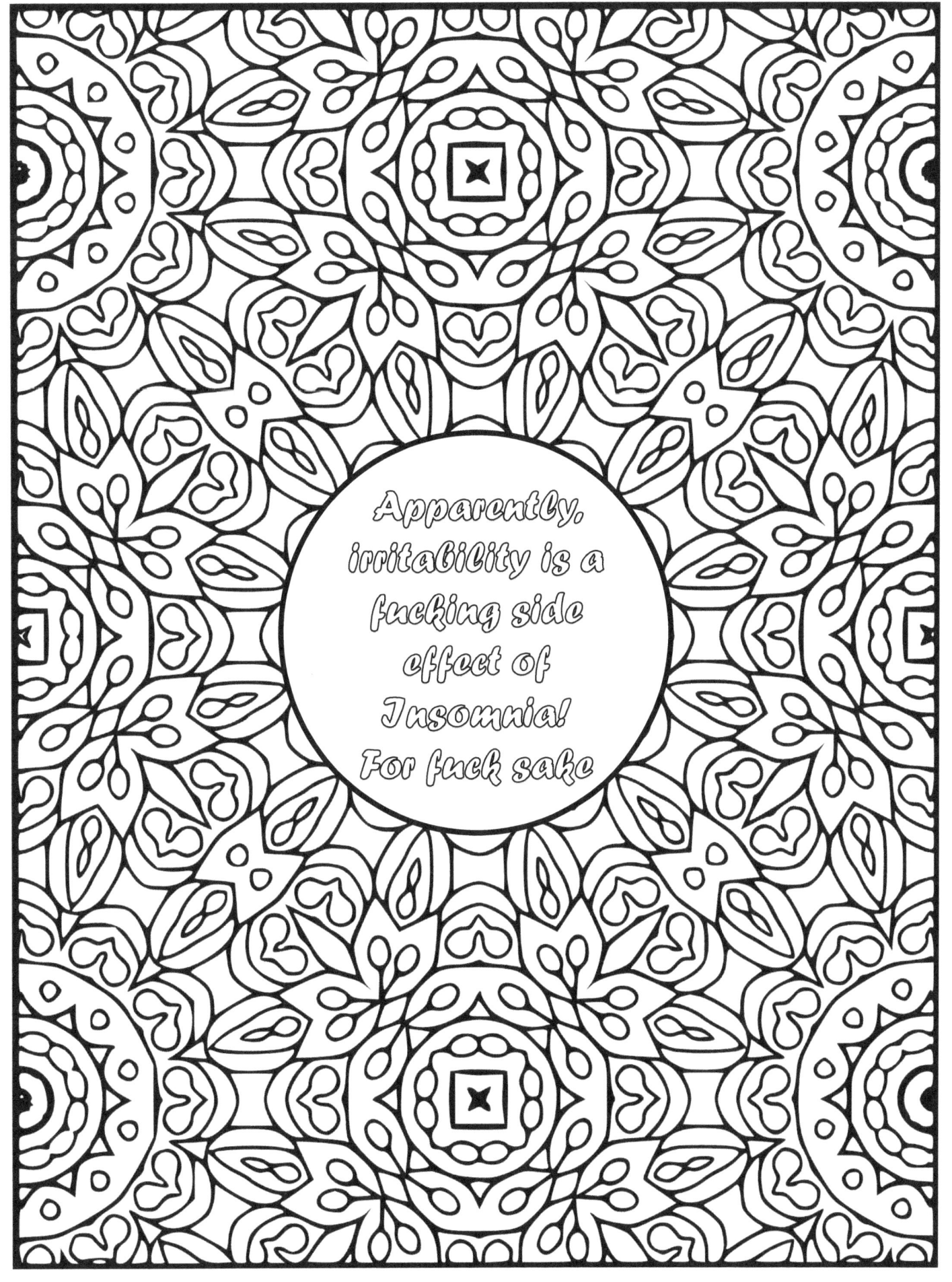

Apparently, irritability is a fucking side effect of Insomnia! For fuck sake

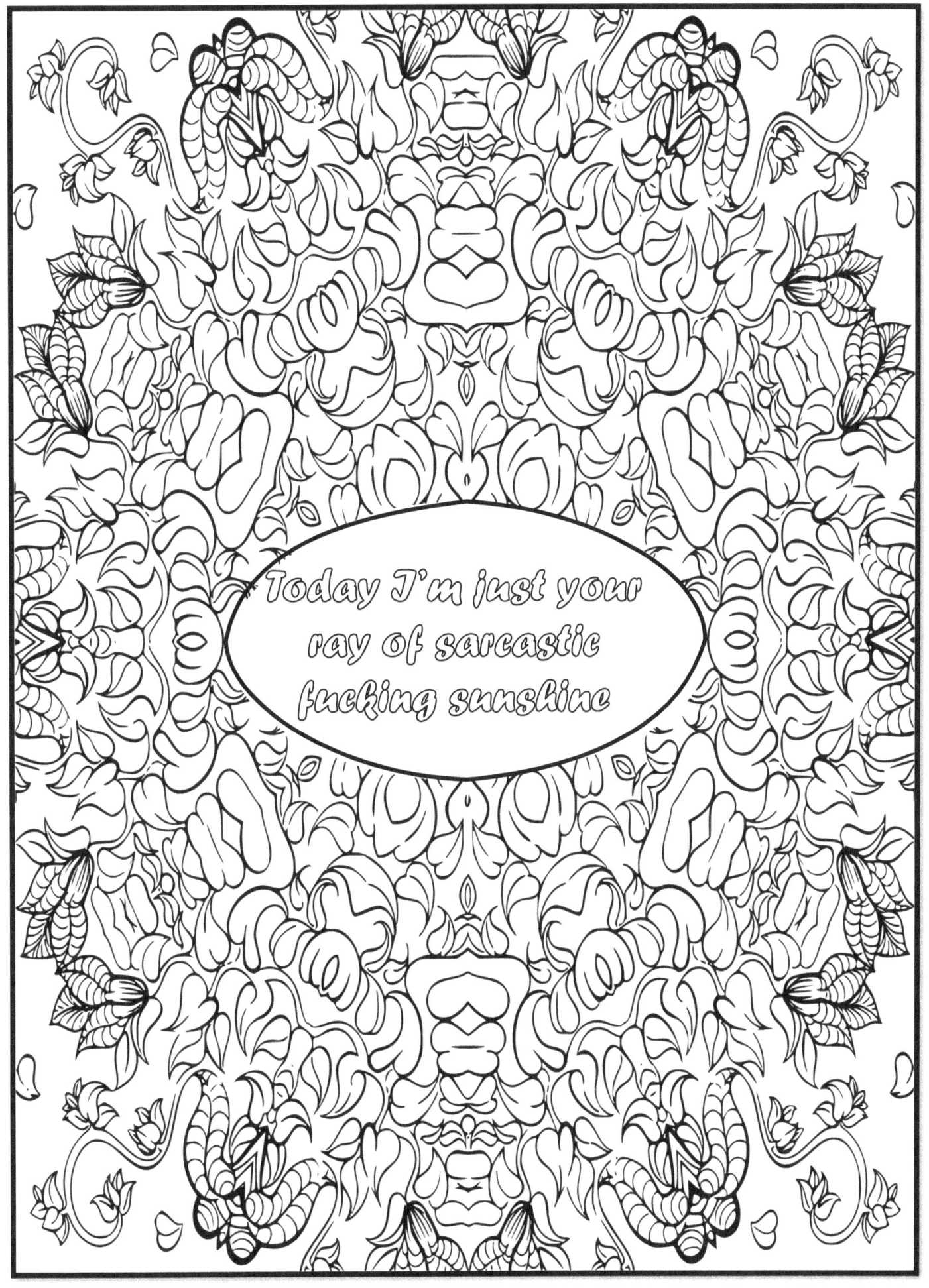

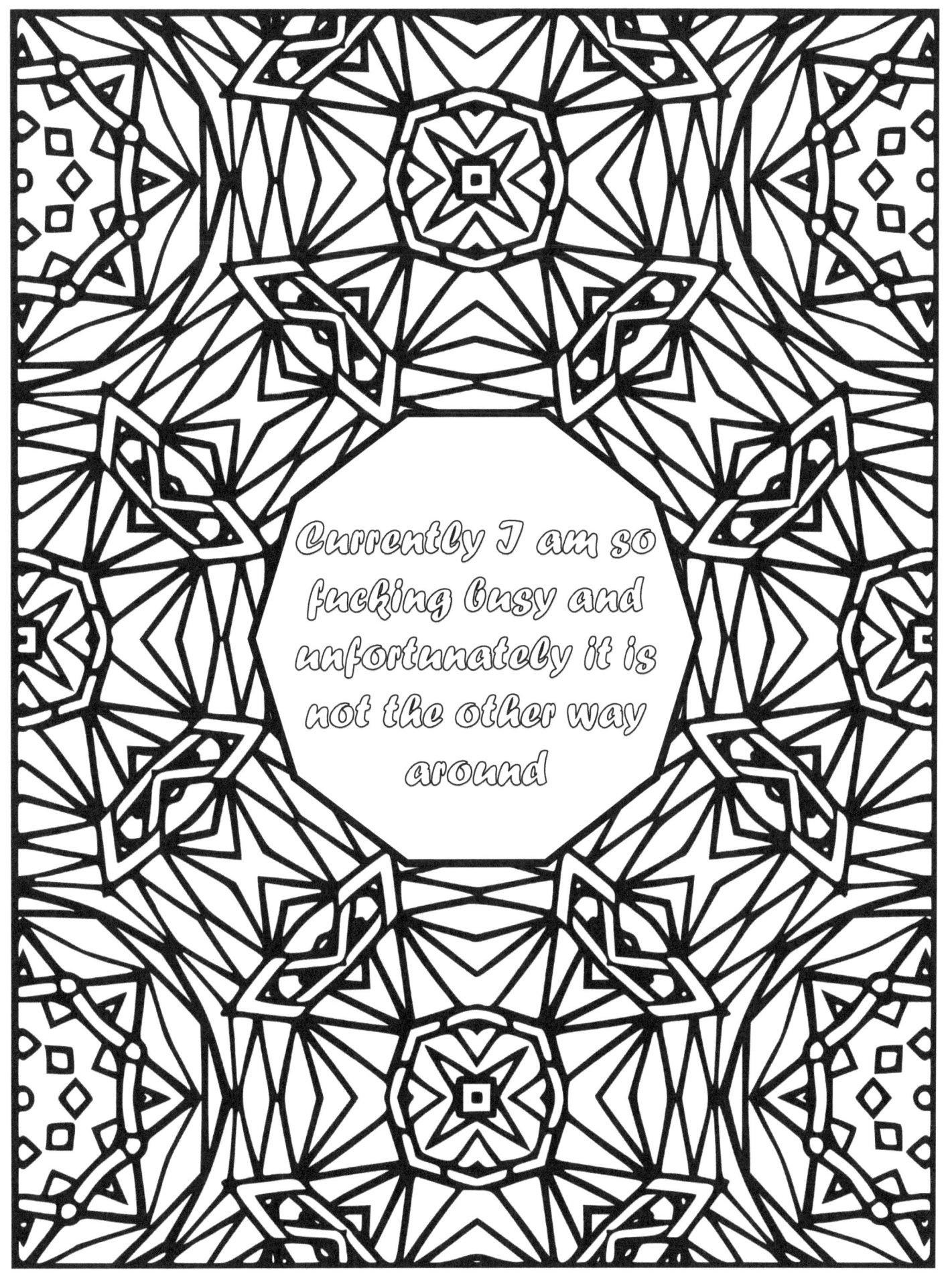